Theology *for* Life

Theology for Life

A Joy-Filled Introduction to Christian Doctrine

RONNI KURTZ

BakerBooks
a division of Baker Publishing Group
Grand Rapids, Michigan

Published by Baker Books
a division of Baker Publishing Group
Grand Rapids, Michigan
BakerBooks.com

Printed in the United States of America

Library of Congress Cataloging-in-Publication Data
Names: Kurtz, Ronni, author
Title: Theology for life : a joy-filled introduction to Christian doctrine / Ronni Kurtz.
Description: Grand Rapids, Michigan : Baker Books, a division of Baker Publishing Group, [2026] | Includes bibliographical references.
Identifiers: LCCN 2025053312 | ISBN 9781540905123 cloth | ISBN 9781493456512 ebook
Subjects: LCSH: Theology, Doctrinal
Classification: LCC BT65 .K87 2026
LC record available at https://lccn.loc.gov/2025053312

All italics in direct Scripture quotations are the author’s emphasis.

Cover design by Dustin Kilgore

Baker Publishing Group publications use paper produced from sustainable forestry practices and postconsumer waste whenever possible.

26 27 28 29 30 31 32 7 6 5 4 3 2 1

To Cohen Haddon

May you grow to behold.
May the theological life cultivate your soul
to apprehend the true, the good, and the beautiful
all grounded in our Triune God and
seen in the face of Jesus Christ.

Contents

Introduction

From Doctrine to Delight

This book is built on a rather simple conviction: One of the most practical things we can do in the Christian life is get an eyeful of the beauty of the Lord. In a world overflowing with to-do lists and self-help manuals, where pragmatism feels like a gravitational pull, giving sustained attention to the glory of the Lord is among the most preeminent ways to cultivate our souls and shape ourselves as persons.

Contemplating the beauty and glory of the Lord might not *feel* practical, if by practical we mean helping to meet some utilitarian goal like getting that promotion or being a better *whatever*. On the contrary, if getting an immediate payoff is the full depth of what it means for something to be useful, then much of theology would be useless. However, if we reconsider what it means for something to be useful and desire more than a shallow behavior or circumstantial modification; if instead we strive for the much more difficult goal of being formed as a person, where we are not merely *modified* but truly *conformed*, then what was once "useless" theology will show to be gloriously purposeful.

For example, take the apostle Paul's instruction for the church in Corinth: "And we all, with unveiled face, beholding the glory of the Lord, are being transformed into the same image from one degree of glory to another. For this comes from the Lord who is the Spirit" (2 Cor. 3:18). Notice Paul's goal for his readers: to be "transformed into the same image from one degree of glory to another." The image Paul is referencing in this vital verse is none other than the image of Christ. Paul wants the Corinthian Christians to not merely modify a few behaviors or become a better version of themselves. Rather, Paul wants them to be *transformed* into the image of Christ. What is easy to miss in this passage, however, is that Paul not only gives the Corinthians a goal—to be transformed into the image of Christ—but also tells them the *way* they will achieve this goal. It is through *beholding the glory of the Lord* that believers will be transformed into the image of Christ.

Beholding is the key intention of Paul in this passage and the key intention of the book you hold in your hands. In a world drowning in meaningless activity, a life characterized by beholding produces wonder and awe. It is not difficult to find a Christian book with a set of specific instructions or a twelve-step plan that promises a better future. However, in line with 2 Corinthians 3, the instruction of this book is rather simple: *Look.* Look at the Triune God and behold. Look at God's beauty until we see it. Look at the Father until his ways are our ways. Look at Christ until he is the treasure worth following to the ends of the earth. Look at the Holy Spirit until we see him as the source of conviction and comfort he is. While the voices of a million lesser loves beckon for our attention, the hope of Christian theology is to turn our mind's eye toward the beauty of the Triune God and behold.

My hope for this book—and, in fact, my hope for the entirety of the Christian theological life—is that we would look *at* Christ until we look *like* Christ. While it may not feel this way at first, giving sustained attention to the beauty of the Triune God will change *everything*. Getting a greater vision of *who* God is and *what* God is up to in the world will indeed transform us. This transformation will come with a myriad of practical payoffs—the most important being that we will be transformed, from one degree of glory to another, into the image of Christ.

If it is Christlikeness we are after, then Christian theology and doctrine are a gift of God.

◇◇◇◇◇

I have mentioned the words *theology* and *doctrine* a few times already, and we will work toward an explicit definition of both in the pages to come. Yet it is important to note here that contemplating the Lord in the task we call Christian theology is not the only way to pursue this transformational beholding of God. While theological and doctrinal wisdom are important ingredients in Christian sanctification, they are not sufficient ingredients. If we want to be truly transformed into the image of Christ, it will take more than theological maturity; it will also necessitate emotional maturity, relational maturity, ecclesial maturity, and much more.

Yet while considering the beauty of Christian theology and the doctrines that make it up might not be sufficient for full Christian maturity, they are still necessary. In my own life, I have experienced the transforming power that comes with sanctified thinking. I have learned that the distance between my heart and my head is not as far as I would have imagined. The more I consider the glory of God in Christian doctrine, the more I love God himself. In this way, theology or doctrine is not the goal; God is the goal. Theology and doctrine are wonderful tools and, when wielded properly, can act as glasses that bring into focus the beauty of the Lord.

Therefore, in this book, we will turn toward Christian doctrine not just to become better thinkers and theologians but with a particular goal in mind: delight. To put it plainly: Delight is what this book is after, and beholding God in Christian doctrine is the intended means to get us there.

Misuses and Abuses of Doctrine and Theology

This book presents a positive vision of Christian doctrine and theology—a vision that sees the invitation of theology as an invitation to marvel and wonder. I am convinced that Christian theology is an endeavor worthy of all our days; it is the kind of exercise, if done well, that will form our souls, give us stability as persons, sanctify our worship, and give us an inexhaustible impetus for worship. However, while theology has the ability, when done as faith seeking understanding, to produce all these wonders in the Christian pilgrim, it is not hard to find examples of theology being used in poor ways and toward unfortunate outcomes.

Theology can be the wicked reversal of Joseph's comfort to his brothers in Egypt. Joseph told his brothers that what they meant for evil, God meant for good; theology done without faithfulness can be an instrument leading in the reverse direction: What God meant for good, they have used for evil (Gen. 50:20).

When theology is used for evil, it often leaves wounds that run deep. Given that bad theology is often done in God's name, by God's people, and includes misusing God's Word, these cuts can both hurt and confuse. God's name, God's people, and God's Word ought to bring about delight and discipleship.

When they are used against Christians, or at least used in a maligning way, the wound is made all the more severe since they are in the stead of what should have been glorious.

There are many ways theology can be misused and abused.[1] Given this book aims to see doctrine as an avenue for delight, articulating ways theology and doctrine may be used for ill may prove helpful and can give us a diagnostic for the way theology moves us in our own time spent contemplating the Lord. Theology done well ought to lead us to delight in the Lord and pursue the good of our neighbor; theology done poorly can lead to many negative outcomes. The three pairs I have in mind here are (1) performance and pride, (2) division and discord, and (3) a poor substitute for wisdom and wholeness.

Performance and Pride

To say that theology can be misused in the direction of performance and pride is to recognize that there are those whose goal is applause, and theology just happens to be a convenient vehicle toward that end. Of course, this ultimate desire is not an expressed one, for few would come out and explicitly state that they strive for applause, yet the gravitational pull toward acceptance via doctrinal thinking is real. There are spaces in evangelicalism where it seems that theology has become something of a stage on which doctrinal pundits perform an act in hopes of riling an already agreeable base toward applause and acceptance. As we have seen various news outlets move from the business of information toward entertainment, we have also

1. There are, of course, others who have written about misuses and abuses of theology. See, for example, the three reasons Keith Johnson gives in his book *Theology as Discipleship* (IVP Academic, 2015), which has some overlap with the three I have listed here. Also see my chapter "Why Do the Theologians Rage?" in Ronni Kurtz, *Fruitful Theology: How the Life of the Mind Leads to the Life of the Soul* (B&H, 2022).

witnessed a growth—especially in our social media age—of theology-as-entertainment in which the goal is not the glory of God or love of our neighbor but the continued pursuit of outrage, clicks, and controversies.

When theology is pursued as a performance, it is often accompanied by pride. There is something intoxicating about receiving the applause of others, being the focal point, memorizing arguments, using fancy jargon, and being the most informed person in a room. When time spent developing theological ability is used toward the end of puffing someone up instead of in service to God and his people, corrosive pride often follows. We know pride has taken over the theological pursuit when the telos, or goal, of our theology shifts from loving our neighbor to getting the attention of our neighbor.

Division and Discord

Beyond the pull toward performance and pride that can accompany theology done poorly is the evergreen worry that theology may lead to division and discord. The worry here is that theological exploration will lead not to intellectual clarity leading to deeper community and more rooted belonging but to an ever-growing list of ideas over which the church may divide. This problem is accentuated by our cultural moment. It seems that some spheres of theological discourse have taken notes from modern political discourse, as many of the same divisive tactics are employed. When theology is framed merely in us-versus-them dynamics, it is easy to prioritize "winning" doctrinal arguments and "defeating opponents." Rather than theological contemplation being a God-ordained means to steady our souls and form us into persons who are equipped and enabled to behold the glory of God, theology done poorly has the potential instead to become mere intellectual ammunition in our ever-shifting ideological wars.

Substitute Wisdom and Wholeness

The final malpractice I want to mention is mistaking theological knowledge for wisdom. To put it plainly: We must see Christian maturity and sanctification as more than mere theological intelligence. When Scripture describes faithful followers of Christ, it seems to have the whole person in mind. For example, when the Synoptic Gospels discuss "the greatest commandment," we can see the emphasis in Matthew's, Mark's, and Luke's lists. The disciples ask Jesus, "Which is the greatest commandment in the law?" In Matthew's account, Jesus says the greatest commandment is to love the Lord with all your heart, all your soul, and all your mind (Matt. 22:36–40). Mark's and Luke's accounts also include these three—heart, soul, mind—but also include a fourth: strength (Mark 12:28–31; Luke 10:27).

Two observations about these passages are important for our purposes: First, any notion of holistic devotion to the Lord *must* include the life of the mind. Theological contemplation is not reserved for a special sect of super-Christians but is the glorious calling and task of all those who wish to follow Christ. Second, while all three lists include the mind, they also include other elements of the Christian life. These two observations come together to instruct us that the life of the mind is a necessary ingredient but is not sufficient for a holistic understanding of Christian maturity.

Yes, theological wisdom is needed for a rooted stability in the Christian life. So is relational wisdom, emotional wisdom, ecclesial wisdom, and more. We must not make the mistake of confusing theological intelligence for Christian wisdom. Knowing a lot of facts *about* God does not mean one has an intimate relationship *with* God. Moreover, knowledge and wisdom are not synonymous. There is a substantial difference between being well-read in theology and knowing how the doctrines that make up the Christian faith cultivate our souls and enable us to administer reality in a world full of lies.

That Leads to Delight

The proper response to theology done poorly cannot be no theology at all. We are a theological people, and turning our mind's eye toward the glory of the Lord is among the highest of delights. Our souls, and our churches, cannot afford a nontheological life. Instead, we will take up the gift that is considering God in theology and bend it toward God's glory, our joy, and the good of our neighbors.

We live in a distracted age, one in which depth of soul is hard to come by. We are a people surrounded by noise, distraction, and shallowness. How vital, then, for the church to have an ever-increasing population who will stop scrolling themselves to death and give their focus to something worthwhile. The church in our era, like in any era, needs those who have done the hard work of pursuing a cultivated soul. We need men and women of depth who can actually give sustained attention to the true, the good, and the beautiful and are convinced this is a proper path toward the good life. We need everyday Christians, not just pastors or professors, who will take up the task of theological discipleship. We must recognize, as John Webster once stated, that "good theology demands good theologians" and that "good theologians are those whose life and thought are caught up in the process of being slain and made alive by the gospel and of acquiring and exercising habits of mind and heart which take very seriously the gospel's provocation."[2]

This is a call for all of us. We all have access to sit at the feet of the Triune God and behold. Behold in such a way that we are conformed from one degree of glory to another; behold in such

2. John Webster, *The Culture of Theology* (Baker Academic, 2019), 133.

a way that the beauty of Christ makes all else in this world seem like lesser loves; behold in such a way that our minds become kindling, kindling that ignites as we contemplate God's glory setting ablaze our affection for God and his people.

We set sail, then, on our journey of examining ten doctrines and theological ideas in the Christian faith, holding them up like precious gems, turning them over this way and that in hopes that we might see the beauty of Christian doctrine. In the end, this exercise will be not just for examination but for exaltation. We hope to move forward into these ten doctrines to show how the Christian intellectual life, especially bound in theological contemplation of God and all things in relation to God, is an invitation to delight.

A Quick Word to the Reader

My aim for this book is the ever-elusive balance between being theologically rich and being accessible for regular, everyday Christians. I do *not* want to shy away from going toward the deep end of the theological pool. I use true theological grammar and invite readers to consider doctrines and ideas they may have never heard before. However, while I am committed to not merely staying at the surface level of Christian theology, I am equally committed to not merely explaining doctrine but seeing that doctrine *exalt* the Lord. Again, we are after exaltation, not mere examination. And so, while we will pursue the deep end of the pool, I'll also give some swimming instructions along the way.

This means there will be sections of the book that may feel a bit denser than some readers are used to reading. If that happens for you, I know this is asking a lot, but stick with me. For every twist and turn considering theological language, there are corresponding sections that seek to show why these doctrines really matter in day-to-day life. For example, some readers may find the most difficult chapters in this book are those covering the doctrines of the Trinity, God's attributes, and the incarnation. This should be no surprise, given the mystery of these three areas of theology and the fact that our aim is to get *into* the weeds of theological thinking instead of merely talking *about* it.

And yes, there will be other readers who will wish this book to be even more in-depth. That is okay as well. My aim in this book is bringing worlds together: the world of substantial contemplation of theological ideas and the world of real people in real local churches. The consequence will be that this book is not for everyone. It is for those who want to bridge these worlds—doctrine and delight—and consider God while also contemplating how these truths about God seep into the deepest places of our souls and transform us.

Readers should be able to see this dual commitment in the structure of each chapter below. Each chapter begins by *defining* a doctrine or theological idea in the first half of the chapter and then moves into *delighting* in the doctrine in the second half. The hope is that the first section will speak to our minds as we pursue not merely talking *about* theology but actually picking up theological ideas and wrestling with them. Then, the second section has our hearts in view, showing that examining doctrine is never an end in itself but an invitation to move from examination to exaltation as we rejoice in our great God and his glorious work.

Defining Four Key Terms

We'll close this introductory chapter by clarifying a few terms that will show up time and again throughout this book. Clarity is a friend to learning, so gaining conceptual clarity about a few pieces of theological grammar will prove useful for the remainder of this book. I have in mind, especially here at the beginning, four terms: *theology*, *theological fields*, *theological loci*, and *doctrine*. While each chapter will introduce new theological grammar important for its topic, these four terms will prove important throughout all chapters.

1. Theology

In some ways, it can be difficult to define theology. This is because, in one sense, *theology* is a word that simply means "thoughts about God" or "speech about God." In another sense, theology is an entire field of study within Christianity that entails vast literature, its own set of vocabulary and methods, and more. As for the simpler side of defining theology, examining the two Greek words that make up the word can be helpful. Those two Greek words are *theos* and *logos*. Keith Johnson helpfully utilizes this method in his definition of theology:

> The word *theology* comes from the Greek term *logos*, often translated as "reason" or "word," and *theos*, which means "God." We practice theology whenever we think or speak about God. We are doing theology when we pray, worship, read Scripture, teach others about the faith and make decisions about how to live in a right relationship to God. In this sense, every Christian practices theology every day.[3]

Picking up from Johnson's last sentence, we can see the inevitability of theology. If theology is simply words about God or thoughts about God, then it would be an impossibility *not* to practice theology, for we all have theological thoughts. Even an atheist who says "There is no God" is practicing theology insomuch as they are speaking words about God, even if false. It is this broad definition of "words or thoughts about God" that leads to the conclusion that all of us, without exception,

3. Johnson, *Theology as Discipleship*, 17.

are theologians. Again, the question is not if we will be theologians. That question has been settled; we *will* do theology. The more pertinent question facing Christians, then, is will we be faithful theologians?

As for our purposes in this book, there is an oft-cited definition of theology that comes from several sources in varying points of church history. The definition of theology we will move forward with is this: *Theology is the study of God and all things in relation to God.* This definition is properly God-centered, meaning it gets not only the definition correct but also the *order* of the material correct. Theology's chief concern is God himself. While theology is also interested in a nearly endless list of other topics, it first concerns itself with God.

We could, of course, talk about a theology of creation, a theology of salvation, a theology of the church, and a theology of the end times (and we will). However, theology first talks of God, as he is the principle of all theological concerns. All things are from him, through him, and will one day go back to him (Rom. 11:36), and so, as the supreme source of all things, God is the supreme subject of theology.

While it is important to keep God as the primary concern and emphasis in theology, know also that God has acted among us. While God would have been infinitely happy in his own triune life, he turns toward us creatures and acts. God has brought about the creation of the cosmos, he has saved a sinful people, he has gathered people up together in the church—he has done more works than all the books of the world could contain (John 21:25) and is still working among us. When considering all God's works, we do so by first considering God and then relating all things back to him as their supreme source and end.

This twofold understanding of theology is repeated throughout church history as a stable way to understand what it means to pursue the theological life. A famous post-Reformation theologian, Francis Turretin, defined the subject of theology by saying, "All things are discussed in theology either because they deal with God himself or have a relation to him as the first principle and ultimate end."[4] Maybe the most well-known articulation of this definition and subject matter of theology comes from the late theologian John Webster, whose influence runs throughout this book. He writes:

> Christian theology is a work of regenerate intelligence, awakened and illuminated by divine instruction to consider a twofold object. This object is, first, God in himself in the unsurpassable perfection of his inner being and work as Father, Son and Spirit and in his outer operations, and, second and by derivation, all other things relative to him.[5]

So then, what is theology? Theology is the profound gift of God, given to all his children, in which we pursue the glorious and fearful task of considering God and all things in relation to God. It is our taking hold of his revelation and trying, even in our feeble efforts, to turn our mind's eye in his direction in hopes that we may behold his glory and in so doing be conformed into the image of Christ from one degree of glory to another (2 Cor. 3:18).

2. Theological Fields

Now that we have a working definition of theology—the study of God and all things in relation to God—we need to differentiate the *kinds* of theology. Often, these various ways of practicing Christian theology are called "fields" or "disciplines."

When thinking of the term *fields of theology*, it may be helpful to compare theology to another discipline of study.

4. Francis Turretin, *Institutes of Elenctic Theology*, vol. 1, ed. James T. Dennison Jr., trans. George Musgrave Giger (P&R, 1992), 16.

5. John Webster, *God Without Measure: Working Papers in Christian Theology*, God and the Works of God, vol. 1 (T&T Clark, 2015), 1.

The discipline of science, for example, can be broken up into subfields such as biology, chemistry, physics, astronomy, and more. Theology is similar. While the four subfields of theology discussed below are all properly called theological, they pursue the task of Christian theology from different places, utilize different tools, and ask different questions.[6] These four fields are biblical theology, historical theology, philosophical theology, and systematic theology.

Theological Fields

Type of Theology	Definition
Biblical Theology	The study of God focused on attending to the development of biblical themes and motifs throughout Scripture
Historical Theology	The study of God focused on attending to the development of Christian thought through individuals, eras, movements, and denominations
Philosophical Theology	The study of God focused on attending to philosophical resources in pursuit of clarity concerning the Christian faith
Systematic Theology	The study of God focused on attending to constructing, connecting, and codifying Christian belief drawn from a variety of sources, including the other three fields of theology

There are many reasons I find it helpful to teach students these various fields of Christian theology. Of the most important, and something I find especially helpful for those still in

6. While I think discussing the fields of theology is a legitimate task, I do have a few caveats I like to put forward regarding the separation of these four fields. First, given that each field is broad and covers many thinkers, theories, and methods, readers may find that other theologians define each of these four fields with varying emphases. Second, I do get weary of splitting the theological task up *too much* and seeing these four fields as silos. Theology is done best when theologians seek to engage all these fields. When a single field pursues the theological task apart from the others, it can be to the detriment of theology. Finally, dividing the labor of Christian theology between these four subfields is not necessarily neat and tidy. Many, if not most, theological inquiries overlap multiple fields. These caveats notwithstanding, understanding the subfields of Christian theology can be a helpful exercise for those early in their theological journey.

the early stages of their theological development, is that understanding the various fields can alleviate pressure to know it all or have all the answers about one's faith.

Here is what I mean: At some point, you are going to come across a question regarding the Christian faith that you do not know how to answer. Whether that question arises from your own Bible reading, a friend, or something you hear in a sermon, the reality is that you cannot (and should not expect yourself to) know *everything* regarding Christianity, and that is okay. Knowing the theological fields and what they focus on will not rid you of your questions but will help you be more informed. When you inevitably come across a question you do not know how to answer, you can say something like, "I do not know the answer to this question, but I do know the answer is likely over *there*."

For example, if someone falsely claims that the Bible is erroneous because there is a fifth Gospel that should be included with Matthew, Mark, Luke, and John, you may not know exactly what to say, but you will know that the answer is likely in *historical theology*. Therefore, you can begin your search for an answer at least heading in the proper direction. Or, if someone tries to stump you with the sophomoric question "If God can do all things, can he make a rock so heavy that he cannot himself lift it?" in hopes that you will believe God's power is a contradiction in itself, you may not know how to answer immediately, but you will be aware that the answer is likely in *philosophical theology*.

Knowing the various fields of Christian theology can help you organize your thoughts and begin to assemble a theological building in your mind, knowing that different rooms will contain different answers. When faced with uncertainty in theology as you come across areas of your own ignorance, you can take a deep breath, know you are okay, be assured that *someone* in the Christian faith has given good thought to this question, and know in which "room" that thought will be found. This moves new questions from the realm of worrisome doubt to theological exploration that ought to lead to joy.

3. Theological Loci

Just as there are various theological fields, there are also various theological subjects. These subjects are sometimes called *theological loci* (which is simply the plural form of the word *locus*), meaning these are "locations" of theology. These subjects within Christian theology often overlap with one another, yet an understanding of the major loci in Christian theology has similar advantages to knowing the fields of theology. Having some knowledge of these subjects, even if it is simply the knowledge that they exist, gives some organization to your mental furniture.

When questions arise surrounding Christian theology, you may not know what the answer is, but you may know the answer is in the realm of soteriology or Christology, for example. Having these working categories gives you the advantage of not eliminating all ignorance but having some *informed* ignorance. The major theological loci in Christian theology often share a pattern when it comes to their names. Most of the major loci are the combination of a Greek root plus the Greek word *logos*, which we have already seen above. In rendering these terms in English, we typically use the English suffix *-ology*, which means something like "the study of." For example, *biology*: *bios* is the Greek word for "life," and when we attach the suffix *-ology*, biology is "the study of life."

An example from theology is the word *soteriology*. The root of this word is the Greek word *soteria*, which gets at the idea of salvation. So, *soteria* plus *-ology* means "the study of salvation." *Pneumatology* is another good example. The Greek word *pneuma* can be rendered "spirit" or "breath"; in this case, it is being used to refer to the Holy Spirit, such that *pneumatology* is "the study of the Holy Spirit." What follows is a table listing some of the major subjects of Christian theology and their most basic definition.

Theological Loci

Theological Locus	Definition
Theology Proper	The study of God in himself, without respect to his work
Soteriology	The study of salvation
Ecclesiology	The study of the church
Eschatology	The study of the last things
Anthropology	The study of humans and society
Paterology	The study of the Father
Christology	The study of the Son
Pneumatology	The study of the Holy Spirit
Hamartiology	The study of sin
Angelology	The study of angels
Bibliology	The study of Scripture

4. Doctrine

Finally, it is important to consider the word *doctrine*. As we navigated through these four key terms, in some ways we started with the largest and moved to the smallest. Theology (1) can be divided into four disciplines (2). These four disciplines treat various theological loci (3). The major theological loci are made up of doctrines (4). Therefore, in simple terms, *doctrine* can be understood as the individual teachings within Christian theology that make up larger theological subjects.

Doctrine acts as the building blocks of the Christian faith. In his kindness, God has spoken to us in his Word, and the task of developing doctrine is our grabbing hold of that speech in faith, attempting to make sense of both it and its speaker. In developing and learning doctrine, we practice that great task of *faith seeking understanding* as we gaze at the beauty of the Lord in hopes of knowing him and seeing his work in our world. Doctrine allows us to put words to our beholding and words to our wonder of the Lord. Moreover, doctrine allows us to preserve biblical fidelity as we seek to pass down the faith from one generation to the next, as we ourselves have received in Scripture the "faith that was once for all delivered to the saints" (Jude 3).

◇◇◇◇◇

Astute readers may look at the table of contents for this book and recognize that some chapters focus on individual doctrines while others focus on loci or full subjects of theology. For example, chapter 6 covers the *doctrine* of justification, while chapter 9 focuses on ecclesiology as a theological *locus*. Having working definitions of doctrine and loci will help us as we advance into those chapters, as one is a single doctrine while the other is a whole field of theology.

Now that the stage has been set, we turn to considering ten doctrines and areas of Christian theology, all with the hope of moving from truth in our heads to delight in our hearts. These ten areas of Christian truth ought to put on display that, despite any caricatures about theology and its misuses we've seen, in the end, we should all pursue *theology for life*.

1

Trinity

Delighting in Your God

The Trinity is not merely one doctrine among others in the Christian faith; in many ways, the Trinity is the very substance of the Christian faith. All that has existed has existed because the Triune God created it out of nothing; all that currently exists does so because the Triune God providentially allows it to be; all that will exist will exist to glorify the Triune God and will find its end in him. This is, of course, just another way to say that all things are "*from him* and *through him* and *to him*" (Rom. 11:36).

Introducing the Doctrine of the Trinity

To say that the Trinity is the substance of the Christian faith is to give God pride of place in our theological imagination. If we return to our table of *-ology* words, we can see this place of preeminence in action. All the words categorized under theological loci find their proper place in reference to the Trinity. For example, it is quite easy to imagine studying the doctrine of the Trinity without reference to salvation, yet it would be impossible to properly study soteriology—or the study of salvation—without reference to the Trinity, since it is the Triune God who redeems a wayward people. Or another example: We could imagine studying the doctrine of the Trinity without reference to the doctrine of the church, yet it would be impossible to properly study ecclesiology—or the study of the church—without reference to the Trinity, since the church is *God's* people.

We could run this example with every doctrine contained in the brief list of theological loci. All of them, without fail, either are directly *about* the Trinity or find their existence *because* of the Trinity. Showing how all Christian theology flows *from* the Trinity calls our minds back to our definition of theology from the introduction and represents the idea that theology really has a twofold subject: the Triune God and all things in relation to the Triune God. In other words, "Either it is God Himself that is the subject, or things that are ordered with respect to God, as to the universal principle and end of those things."[1]

One last thing worth mentioning before we dive into defining and delighting in the doctrine of the Trinity: Since we are in the realm of "theology proper" (or that which is properly about God in himself) in this chapter and the next, readers ought to be aware that these subjects can sometimes feel more difficult than others, and rightly so. The thing we seek to define and delight in is none other than God himself. So, if we feel as if the task is difficult or out of our reach, that means we are on the right track. Any god easy to describe and understand

1. Franciscus Junius, *A Treatise on True Theology: With the Life of Franciscus Junius*, trans. David C. Noe (Reformation Heritage Books, 2014), 178. Or, as Junius states in his twenty-fourth thesis on true theology: "The material of this theology consists of divine matters: of course, God, and whatsoever topics have been arranged with respect to Him, as was proper for instruction to be given concerning the nature, works, and law of God Himself." *Treatise on True Theology*, 177.

would be too small to worship. The Triune God of the Bible "dwells in unapproachable light" (1 Tim. 6:16), and "his greatness is unsearchable" (Ps. 145:3). This is simply my warning that chapters 1 and 2 may tackle some ideas and words that seem difficult to those just beginning their theological journey. If that is you, might I ask you to hang with me? I would like to introduce some ideas and theological grammar that, while they may be new, might enable you to better know and love your God. Once we move from theology proper into the economic realm of theology (salvation, the church, eschatology, and so on) in chapters 3 through 10, the terms and ideas will hopefully be a touch more attainable even for beginning theologians.

With that said, we turn now to consider not one doctrine among others but the preeminent teaching in the Christian faith: God himself, our treasure, our prize, and our *ultimate delight*.

Defining the Doctrine of the Trinity

The Christian doctrine of the Trinity is a confession of both *oneness* and *threeness*. As contradictory as it can seem at first glance, Christians confess that God is both—at the same time—one and three. We believe God is *one* because he is one essence; we believe God is *three* because God is three persons—the Father, the Son, and the Holy Spirit.

This basic confession of both oneness and threeness is a good start toward getting at the church's confession of the Triune God. If we want to build a more robust statement about what the church believes about the Trinity, it may sound something like this:

> We worship one God in Trinity and the Trinity in unity, neither confounding their persons nor dividing the essence. For the person of the Father is a distinct person, the person of the Son

> is another, and that of the Holy Spirit still another. But the divinity of the Father, Son, and Holy Spirit is one, the glory equal, the majesty coeternal. Such as the Father is, such is the Son and such is the Holy Spirit. . . . The Father is eternal, the Son is eternal, the Holy Spirit is eternal. And yet there are not three eternal beings; there is but one eternal being. . . . Thus, the Father is God, the Son is God, the Holy Spirit is God. Yet there are not three gods; there is but one God. . . . None in this Trinity is before or after, none is greater or smaller; in their entirety the three persons are coeternal and coequal with each other. So in everything, as was said earlier, the unity in Trinity, and the Trinity in unity, is to be worshiped.[2]

This paragraph is, of course, a portion of the Athanasian Creed—an ancient creed that has been used for centuries in Christianity to help summarize some of the major points of trinitarian theology. This paragraph is riddled with beauty and truth concerning God's triunity. I often tell students a short clause like "neither confounding their persons nor dividing the essence" will save them from a whole host of trinitarian difficulties and mistakes. We, along with the Christian tradition, believe that God is one, as he declares in the ever-important passage of Deuteronomy 6:4: "Hear, O Israel: The LORD our God, the LORD is *one*." We believe not in three gods but in one God. As a result, Christianity is truly a monotheistic religion (belief in a single God). Yet, what makes it different from other monotheistic religions like Judaism and Islam is that while our God is one in essence, that one essence subsists in three divine persons. (More on this phrase in a bit.)

The doctrine of the Trinity can feel like an impossible mountain to climb. In fact, it is. We will never scale to the heights of all that it means for God to be triune, as his three-in-oneness

2. Chad Van Dixhoorn, ed., "The Athanasian Creed," in *Creeds, Confessions, and Catechisms* (Crossway, 2022), 19.

will always be just out of reach of our creaturely words and our ability to fully comprehend. Nevertheless, because God has graciously revealed himself in his Word, we can take hold of Scripture and work on our biblical reading and biblical reasoning to know and name this glorious Triune God.

I want to explore defining the Trinity in two sections to follow: First, I want to show the Trinity's unique place in Scripture. In short, the Trinity is not a doctrine that is merely proven by pointing to chapter and verse like other doctrines; the Trinity gives the very shape and structure to the entire Bible. Second, I want to discuss the theological grammar of oneness and threeness. In this second section, we will move from biblical reasoning toward theological reasoning in hopes of showing two doctrines that the church has used for centuries to understand how it is possible for God to be, at the same time, one and three.

How the Trinity Is Revealed in Scripture

Theologian Fred Sanders has helped readers work toward understanding what it means for the Scriptures to proclaim the doctrine of the Trinity.[3] Among the many helpful things readers will find in Sanders's work on the Trinity is the idea that when it comes to seeing the Trinity in Scripture, there is a way we can say that the doctrine of the Trinity is both *less revealed* and *more revealed* than other doctrines. While this comes across as a contradiction upon first glance, understanding what Sanders means in calling the Trinity both *more* and *less* revealed will help us have a robustly biblical understanding of God's triunity.

3. See, for example, Fred Sanders, *The Triune God* (Zondervan, 2016). Sanders is far from alone in producing helpful contemporary resources on how the Scripture teaches the doctrine of the Trinity. For example, see also Scott Swain, *The Trinity: An Introduction* (Crossway, 2020), 25–53; Scott Swain, *The Trinity and the Bible: On Theological Interpretation* (Lexham Press, 2021); Brandon Smith, ed., *The Trinity in the Canon: A Biblical, Theological, Historical, and Practical Proposal* (B&H Academic, 2023); Brandon Smith, *The Biblical Trinity: Encountering the Father, Son, and Holy Spirit in Scripture* (Lexham Press, 2023).

What Sanders means by saying the doctrine is *less revealed* than other doctrines is that some aspects of the Trinity are not immediately chapter-and-verse-able. While we *can* point to individual passages that list all three persons of the Trinity, such as Jesus's command to baptize in the name of the Father, Son, and Spirit (Matt. 28:19), we will not be able to simply proof text our way into a robust Christian affirmation that God is one essence who exists in three persons. For a developed doctrine of the Trinity, we need not only surface-level biblical *reading* but also a deeper and mature biblical *reasoning*.

However, while the doctrine is *less revealed* than other doctrines in this way, in a more significant way we can argue that the doctrine of the Trinity is *more revealed* than other doctrines. For example, Sanders tells us, "In order to inform us that the Father has a Son and a Holy Spirit, the Father sent the Son and the Holy Spirit in person. The triunity of God was revealed when the persons of the Trinity became present among us in new ways, showing up in person and becoming the object of our human observation." He concludes by saying, "In the fullness of time, God did not give us facts about himself, but gave us himself in the person of the Father who sent, the Son who was sent, and the Holy Spirit who was poured out. These events were accompanied by verbally inspired explanatory words; but the latter depend on the former."[4]

To elaborate a bit on Sanders's vital point, the chart below shows that the persons *uniquely* show up. The Father speaks and creation is formed, the Son takes on flesh and becomes Immanuel ("God with us") in the incarnation, and the Holy Spirit descends at Pentecost. These three movements—creation, incarnation, Pentecost—are events wherein the persons of the Trinity show up among creatures in an observable way. While we do have some specific Scriptures that attest to the doctrine

4. Sanders, *Triune God*, 40.

of the Trinity (as we will see below), it is the Trinity that gives shape to the whole canon of Scripture.

Person	Father	Son	Spirit
Event	Creation	Incarnation	Pentecost
Scripture	Genesis 1–2	Matthew 1:18–25 Luke 2:1–7 John 1:1–18	John 14:26 John 15:26 John 16:7 Acts 2:1–41

The Trinity Is Revealed Progressively

Before we leave this first point on how the Trinity is revealed in Scripture, it will prove important to cover one more doctrine that illuminates a biblical doctrine of the Trinity, the doctrine of *progressive revelation*. In short, progressive revelation teaches us that—in his infinite wisdom—God decided not to reveal all things *at once*. Rather, as God reveals both himself and his economy of redemption in Scripture, he does so bit by bit, unfolding a cosmic drama that has something to say to us all. This is why Scripture can use phrases like "at the *right time* Christ died for the ungodly" and "when the *fullness of time* had come, God sent forth his Son" (Rom. 5:6; Gal. 4:4).

Few thinkers have been more helpful to me personally in understanding progressive revelation than the old Princeton theologian B. B. Warfield. Warfield compares the way the Trinity is progressively revealed in Scripture to a dark room becoming illumined:

> The Old Testament may be likened to a chamber richly furnished but dimly lighted; the introduction of light brings into it nothing which is not in it before; but it brings out into clearer view much of what is in it but was only dimly or even not at all perceived before. The mystery of the Trinity is not revealed in the Old Testament; but the mystery of the Trinity underlies

> the Old Testament revelation, and here and there almost comes into view. Thus the Old Testament revelation of God is not corrected by the fuller revelation that follows it, but only perfected, extended and enlarged.[5]

Warfield calls readers to imagine a furnished room with the lights off. To take him up on his example, imagine entering a room you have never been in before, and it is pitch-black. Let us imagine it is a reading room; while you cannot see them, there are a few bookshelves lined with books, a few reading chairs, and a side table or two. As you step inside, you reach out your hand to feel your way through the darkness. Your hand slides over some wood, and you gather there must be a piece of furniture there; as you try to make sense of your surroundings, you may accidentally bump your hip into a few corners.

Now, imagine that someone hears you in that reading room, opens the door, and turns the lights on. You look around at all the furniture that was always there but now is clear to you. Nothing in the room has substantially changed—all the furniture before you now was always present. The difference is that because of the introduction of light in the room, all that was previously there has been revealed to you. This is quite a helpful analogy for the way the Father, Son, and Spirit are progressively revealed in Scripture; the three persons are not revealed all at once yet are *always* there nevertheless.

The persons of the Trinity are made explicitly known to us as they are progressively revealed in their actions and missions among us. We learn about the Father explicitly when he creates, we learn about the Son explicitly when he takes on flesh and dwells among us, and we learn about the Spirit explicitly when he is poured out on the church at Pentecost. This does

5. B. B. Warfield, *The Biblical Doctrine of the Trinity*, vol. 2 (Baker Books, 2003), 141–42.

not mean, however, that the Son and the Spirit were not there throughout the unfolding narrative of the Old Testament. Like the furniture in that dark room, they were always there. In fact, as we read through the Old Testament, we may even find ourselves bumping into them from time to time. We run into phrases like "the Spirit of God was hovering over the face of the waters" (Gen. 1:2) and "by his wounds we are healed" (Isa. 53:5 NIV), and when the "lights" of the New Testament are turned on, we see that we were bumping into the Son and the Spirit, who were there all along.

Individual Passages on the Trinity

While the Trinity is not proven with a few proof texts here and there but rather gives the entire Bible its structure, it is still important to recognize that there are indeed individual passages that seem to be brief but significant articulations of the Trinity. For example, let's consider Galatians 4:4–7, Titus 3:4–7, and 1 Peter 1:1–2 in turn.

> But when the fullness of time had come, God sent forth his Son, born of a woman, born under the law, to redeem those who were under the law, so that we might receive adoption as sons. And because you are sons, God has sent the Spirit of his Son into our hearts, crying, "Abba! Father!" So you are no longer a slave, but a son, and if a son, then an heir through God. (Gal. 4:4–7)

It is easy to miss, in a quick reading of this passage, that all three persons of the Trinity are present even in a single clause. Look again at verse 6: "God [the first person] has sent the Spirit [the third person] of his Son [the second person] into our hearts." This passage will show up later—especially in our chapter on union with Christ—because it not only gives a quick proclamation of the Trinity but also shows how our very salvation has a trinitarian shape.

> But when the goodness and loving kindness of God our Savior appeared, he saved us, not because of works done by us in righteousness, but according to his own mercy, by the washing of regeneration and renewal of the Holy Spirit, whom he poured out on us richly through Jesus Christ our Savior, so that being justified by his grace we might become heirs according to the hope of eternal life. (Titus 3:4–7)

Like the Galatians passage, Titus 3:4–7 gives us a robust trinitarian account of salvation: God (the first person) has cleansed us by the regeneration of the Holy Spirit (the third person), whom he poured out on us through Jesus Christ (the second person).

We can even see testimony to the triunity of the Lord when the apostles write the greetings of their letters. For example, while it is easy to miss, hear how robustly trinitarian the opening of 1 Peter is:

> Peter, an apostle of Jesus Christ, to those who are elect exiles of the dispersion in Pontus, Galatia, Cappadocia, Asia, and Bithynia, according to *the foreknowledge of God the Father, in the sanctification of the Spirit, for obedience to Jesus Christ* and for sprinkling with his blood: May grace and peace be multiplied to you. (1 Pet. 1:1–2)

While there are other examples to which we could point, for brevity's sake, one more will have to suffice. We can see the Trinity closely connected to baptism in the Christian faith. First, we can consider Christ's baptism, in which all three persons are present as the Son is being baptized, the Spirit descends like a dove, and the Father says, "This is my beloved Son, with whom I am well pleased" (Matt. 3:17). While Christ's own baptism is a strong testimony to God's triune nature, it is not just *his* baptism that demonstrates the Trinity. The glory of the Trinity is interwoven into how our Lord instructs *us* to baptize others: "All authority in heaven and on earth has been given to me. Go therefore and make disciples of all nations, baptizing them in *the name of the Father and of the Son and of the Holy Spirit*, teaching them to observe all that I have commanded you. And behold, I am with you always, to the end of the age" (28:18–20).

Not only does Jesus demand that we have the Trinity in our mouths as we baptize people into the Christian faith, but his instruction also gives us another important aspect of the doctrine of the Trinity: oneness and threeness. Notice that Jesus instructs us to baptize in the *name* of the Father, the Son, and the Holy Spirit. The Greek word used here for "name" is *onoma*, and it is in the singular. Yet, while we are to baptize in the *singular name*, Jesus lists *three names*—the Father, the Son, and the Holy Spirit. It is as if, to truly know this God, we must make sense of how these three divine persons can be called by a singular name.

The Grammar of One and Three

Given all the Bible has to say about God, to be faithful Bible readers, Christians must affirm those texts that indicate the *oneness* of God while also affirming that the Father, Son, and Holy Spirit are all God. When we affirm the *oneness* of God, it cannot be to the jeopardy of the fact that this one God is tri-personal; when we affirm the *threeness* of God, it cannot be to the neglect of his unity. This question of how God can be both one and three has been the impetus for centuries of contemplation in the church. It is why Herman Bavinck, a twentieth-century Dutch theologian, once stated, "The deepest question in every Christian confession and dogmatics is this: How can God be one and, nevertheless, three?"[6]

6. Herman Bavinck, *Reformed Dogmatics*, vol. 2, ed. John Bolt (Baker Academic, 2004), 333.

When teaching students about the need to develop a Christian doctrine of the Trinity that does justice to God's being both *one* and *three*, I have found this simple and oft-used chart to be of help.

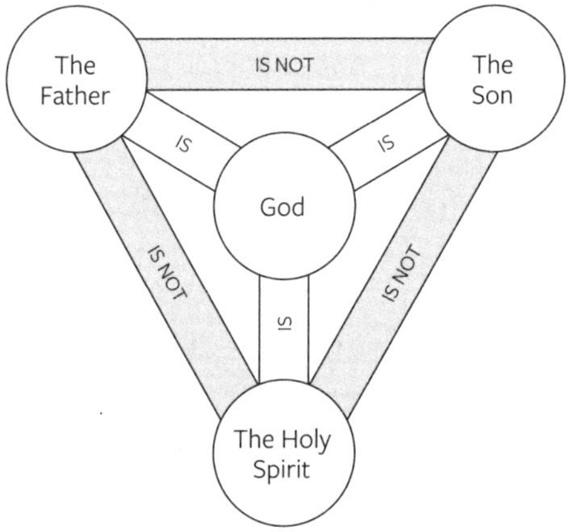

In my experience, most Christians do not have a hard time affirming *that* the Father, the Son, and the Holy Spirit are all God. There is often more confusion, however, with *how* we should affirm their divinity while considering both oneness and threeness. What I have found is that while the chart makes sense for most Christians at a surface level, many struggle to identify what doctrine or biblical truths make the "is" and the "is not" lines of the chart true.

Put another way: What doctrine makes the idea true that the Father, the Son, and the Holy Spirit *are all God*? Also, what doctrine makes the idea true that the Father, the Son, and the Holy Spirit *are not* each other?

On this quest of finding the right kind of grammar to speak about the Trinity, we would be wise to turn an ear to church history. Throughout multiple centuries and across multiple continents, the church has been maturing her confession of God's triune life. Listen to how the notions of one and three show up in fourth-century Africa as Augustine writes,

> The Trinity, one God, of whom are all things, through whom are all things, in whom are all things. Thus, the Father and the Son and the Holy Spirit, and each of these by Himself, is God, and at the same time they are all one God; and each of them by Himself is a complete substance, and yet they are all one substance. The Father is not the Son nor the Holy Spirit; the Son is not the Father nor the Holy Spirit; the Holy Spirit is not the Father nor the Son: but the Father is only Father, the Son is only Son, and the Holy Spirit is only Holy Spirit. To all three belong the same eternity, the same unchangeableness, the same majesty, the same power.[7]

Doing theology in the twenty-first century means we have the deep blessing of inheriting a cosmic conversation about our Lord that spans over two thousand years. If we can tune ourselves to the frequency of that conversation, we will find God has been kind to provide us with a long line of godly men and women who have given sustained attention to articulating our confession. From early church councils, to individual theologians, to the confessions of the church, the doctrine of the Trinity has been the cause for a substantial body of thought and literature. If we were to excavate that body of thought and that body of literature, we would come face-to-face with a staggering amount of beauty—doctrines upon doctrines that aid a faithful reading of the Bible and a faithful confession of God and all things in relation to God.

While it would be a worthwhile project in itself to do that kind of excavation, I want to focus our attention here on two

7. Augustine, "On Christian Doctrine," in *Nicene and Post-Nicene Fathers of the Christian Church*, vol. 2, ed. Philip Schaff (Christian Literature Company, 1887), 524.

of these doctrines: (1) *homoousia*, and (2) the eternal relations of origin. These two doctrines play an important role in church history, and the history around each is vast. I will attempt here not to force a mastery of either idea upon you but rather to bring them into reach so they might play a role in developing your trinitarian imagination and confession. I am convinced that these two doctrines can help us not only have a little more confidence when affirming the doctrine of the Trinity but also make sense of numerous biblical passages. These two doctrines aid us with our language of "one" and "three" by helping us better articulate how God is one in essence and three in persons.

God Is One: The Doctrine of *Homoousia*

It would be hard to exaggerate how important a role the word *homoousia* has played in church history. On face value, it is not overly difficult to understand. *Homoousia* is a theological word that combines two Greek words: *homos* ("same") and *ousia* ("essence" or "substance"). So, *homoousia*, in its most basic form, simply means "same substance."

Readers familiar with church history may know that this word played a significant role in the trinitarian controversies that led up to and came after the Council of Nicaea in AD 325. While many individuals were involved in the trinitarian controversies of this era, two figures worth noting are a priest (Arius) and his bishop (Alexander) from the city of Alexandria. Here is how historian Lewis Ayres chronicles the dispute between the two:

> Alexander taught that God was always Father and that the Son was always Son, thus implying the eternal generation of the Son; as the Father's Word and Wisdom the Son must always have been with the Father. At the same time, he taught that the Son is the exact image of the Father and thus able to reveal and represent him. Arius saw his bishop's theology as implying

> two ultimate principles in the universe, and he thought that Alexander compromised the biblical insistence on the Father's being alone God and alone immortal (1 Tim. 6:16). For Arius, any talk about Father and Son as coeternal ignored the hierarchy involved in the very language of Father and Son. Arius saw the Son as a being distinct from and inferior to the Father, and he seems to have played down metaphorical language that suggested continuity of being or existence between Father and Son. The Son imaged the Father, but only by being created as a derivative copy of some of the Father's attributes.[8]

Arius and Alexander diverged in how each viewed Jesus in relationship to the Father. For Arius, Jesus was an inferior being, a creature who was created by the Father and not one who is eternal like the Father. For Alexander, Jesus was God and all that it entailed to be God; Jesus was coeternal and one with the Father.

While there is much history worth delving into, the point here is not to chronicle the history and positions surrounding the Nicene Council but rather to bring one of its conclusions to light. Arius and those who were persuaded by his arguments argued that Jesus's relationship with the Father is best described as *homoiousia*, whereas Alexander and those who agreed with him argued that Jesus's relationship with the Father is best described as *homoousia*. Notice how similar these words are—only the Greek letter *i* (or *iota*) separates them—yet the difference between the two is the difference between orthodoxy and heresy.

We have already said that *homoousia* means "same substance." If you add that single letter—*i*—the prefix changes to mean "similar" or "like." Therefore, Arius and his followers, who became known as the Arians, taught that Jesus was

8. Lewis Ayres, *Nicaea and Its Legacy: An Approach to Fourth-Century Trinitarian Theology* (Oxford University Press, 2006), 16.

homoiousia with the Father. They believed that while Jesus could be considered divine in some sense of the word, he was not the same kind of divinity as the Father. Jesus was not one with the Father but instead similar in substance to the Father. In the Arian view, the Father is the Creator of all things, and Jesus is the greatest of his creatures, but he is nevertheless on the creaturely side of the Creator-creature divide.

Alexander and his supporters argued that this was an insufficient way to make sense of all the Bible has to say about Jesus. It is better to proclaim that Jesus is *homoousia*—that is, Jesus is *the same substance* as the Father, not just a similar substance. Whatever the Father is, the Son is likewise; he is "very God of very God," as the Nicene Creed says. If the Father is eternal, the Son is eternal; if the Father is all-powerful, the Son is all-powerful.

The dispute was taken up at the Council of Nicaea in AD 325. After about a month of deliberation, the pro-Nicene thinkers agreed that the best way to summarize what the Bible says about Christ is that he is *of one substance*, or *homoousia*, with the Father.

The council, codifying its conclusions, wrote that the Son is:

> God of God, Light of Light,
> Very God of very God;
> Begotten, not made,
> Being of *one substance* with the Father.[9]

Back to our chart above, then: While many doctrines instruct, one doctrine that helps us understand the "is" lines—that the Father, Son, and Holy Spirit are all God—is *homoousia*. All three persons of the Trinity are *one* substance, one essence. There are not three beings or three essences in the

9. "The Nicene Creed," in *Creeds, Confessions, and Catechism*, 17–18.

Trinity. Rather, there is a single essence, and that single essence is God.

God Is Three: The Doctrine of the Eternal Relations of Origin

While *homoousia* helps us make sense of the "is" lines and shows how God is one, what makes the "is not" lines true? Or, to put it another way, how is the Father *not* the Son, and the Son *not* the Spirit, and the Spirit *not* the Son or the Father?

We can start by saying there are many ways we should *not* try to distinguish the three persons of the Godhead. Since the Father, Son, and Holy Spirit are one in essence, we should not try to distinguish their persons in a way that threatens the unity of essence. So, we should *not* articulate the uniqueness of each divine person by saying they have their own wills, their own centers of consciousness, their own powers, or their own authority and submission. On the contrary, by virtue of the three persons being *one*, they share a singular divine essence, a singular divine will, and a singular divine power. Protecting this feature of trinitarian theology will safeguard our claim that Christianity is a monotheistic religion that believes God is one (Deut. 6:4).

And yet, with all that makes them one, we still need a way to meaningfully distinguish between the persons of the Godhead since they are not one another. There is only one Father, only one Son, and only one Holy Spirit. So, how are we to distinguish between the persons of the Trinity without compromising the vital teaching that the Lord is one?

While it has been called different names at various times, the doctrine that helps us meaningfully distinguish between the three persons without compromising their oneness is today called the *eternal relations of origin*. While this doctrine may sound intimidating at first, we can see what it is getting at by taking each part of the name in turn: The doctrine of the eternal relations of origin discusses how the three persons eternally relate to one another. As Scott Swain notes, these relations make sense of the personal names of God:

> The personal names of "Father," "Son," and "Spirit" indicate the mutual relations in which the three stand toward one another, specifically, the personal names indicate *relations of origin*. The Father is Father *to* the Son, who is his "only begotten." The Spirit is spirit *of* the Father and *of* the Son, who is breathed forth in their mutual delight and who displays the glory of their mutual love.[10]

The Father is the unbegotten, the Son is eternally begotten from the Father, and the Spirit eternally proceeds from the Father and the Son. These doctrines get at the "from-ness" for each person: The Father is from no one, the Son is from the Father, the Spirit is from the Father and the Son. However, it is vital to make sure that we do not articulate a hierarchy when discussing this "from-ness." The Son's being from the Father does not make the Father greater than the Son, for while it is true there is no Son without the Father, there is also no Father without the Son. The three persons are the same in their attributes, the same in their glory, the same in being worthy of worship. In fact, they are the same in *every* way except this one way: the way they eternally relate to one another.[11] The Father is always Father, the Son is always Son, and the Spirit is always Spirit.

To end this section, allow me to give a quick word about each of the eternal relations. First, as mentioned, the Father is

10. Scott Swain, "Divine Trinity," in *Christian Dogmatics: Reformed Theology for the Church Catholic*, ed. Michael Allen and Scott Swain (Baker Academic, 2016), 88.

11. As Boethius says, "Hence only terms belonging to relation may be applied singly to Each. For the Father is not the same as the Son, nor is either of Them the same as the Holy Spirit. Yet Father, Son, and Holy Spirit are each the same God, the same in justice, in goodness, in greatness, and in everything that can be predicated of substance." (Boethius, *The Theological Tractates* [Harvard University Press, 1968], 29.)

the unbegotten. This means that no one gives the Father life. The Father is not generated like the Son and does not proceed like the Spirit; rather, the Father is the one who generates the Son and who, with the Son, eternally sends forth the Spirit. An important theological and biblical word we can use to understand the uniqueness of the Father is *paternity*. This word may be familiar as it comes from the Latin word *pater*, meaning "father," and has several fairly common uses in English. When we say the first person of the Trinity is *paternity*, this communicates the unique existence of the first person. He is the fullness of the divine essence as paternity. It is his paternity that separates him from the second and third persons of the Trinity.

As for the second person—the Son—he is eternally generated or begotten from the Father. It is important to separate in our minds the notion of begotten from "created." As the Nicene Creed says, the Son is "begotten, not made." The importance of the distinction between these two is hard to overstate, as one is orthodox Christianity and the other is Arianism. The second person of the Trinity is truly begotten (John 3:16). Yet the Son's being begotten—or his being *from* the Father—is *eternal*. Another word for begotten is *generated*, and likewise, the Son is eternally generated from the Father. The Father ever communicates the divine essence to the Son, and the Son is all the Father is, except he exists not as paternity but as *filiation*, or sonship (John 5:26).

We ourselves have been generated or begotten from our parents, but we can put a time stamp on our generation. There was a time before and after we were generated. It is not this way with the Son. Rather, his generation is an eternal generation. As the Father ever generates the Son, he is ever the Father. As the Son is ever generated from the Father, he is ever the Son. Therefore, there was never a time when the Son was not. As the Father is eternal, the Son is eternal.

Finally, the Holy Spirit eternally proceeds from the Father and the Son. If we carefully read Jesus's words in the upper room discourse in John 13–17, especially 14:26; 15:26; and 16:7, we see testimony to the fact that the Father and the Son send the Holy Spirit, who descends in Acts 2 at Pentecost. This temporary mission—that is, something the persons of the Trinity do *in time*—reflects an eternal reality. Namely, that the Holy Spirit is ever from the Father and the Son. From all eternity, the Father and the Son breathe forth, or *spirate*, the Holy Spirit. The Spirit can be called "the Spirit of the Father" (Matt. 10:20; Rom. 8:11; 1 Cor. 2:11) and also "the Spirit of the Son" (Acts 16:7; Rom. 8:9; Gal. 4:6; Phil. 1:19; 1 Pet. 1:11), as both the Father and the Son forever send the Holy Spirit.

A final point about these terms: While some may think that the theological grammar of the Trinity and theological terms like *unbegotten*, *eternal generation*, *eternal procession*, *spiration*, and so on are too theological and too far removed from the actual language of the Bible, it is easy to miss that these terms simply describe the common biblical titles of Father, Son, and Spirit. We believe, as Christians, that these titles *mean* something and are God's revealed names. We are not free, for example, to refer to the Trinity as "the three brothers" or "the three best friends." Rather, we refer to them by their revealed names of Father, Son, and Spirit. Nineteenth-century Presbyterian theologian William Shedd makes this point in an accessible way that is worth quoting here:

> The trinal names *Father*, *Son*, and *Spirit*, given to God in Scripture, force upon the theologian the ideas of paternity, filiation, spiration, and procession. He cannot reflect upon the implication of these names without forming these ideas and finding himself necessitated to concede their literal validity and objective reality. He cannot say with Scripture that the first person is the Father and then deny or doubt that he "fathers." He cannot

> say that the second person is the Son and then deny or doubt that he is "begotten." He cannot say that the third person is the Spirit and then deny or doubt that he "proceeds" by "spiration" (Spirit because spirated) from the Father and the Son. Whoever accepts the nouns *Father*, *Son*, and *Spirit* as conveying absolute truth must accept also the corresponding adjectives and predicates—beget and begotten, spirate and proceed—as conveying absolute truth.[12]

Let us bring the many points of this chapter together in one chart.

Biblical Claim	Number in Mind	Doctrine That Protects the Idea	Meaning and Emphasis
God is one.	There is *one* substance.	*Homoousia*	All three persons are the *same substance* and the *same essence*—the divine. All three *are* God.
God is three.	There are *three* persons.	Eternal relations of origin	All three persons have different eternal relations of origin: • The Father is unbegotten. • The Son is eternally generated by the Father. • The Spirit eternally proceeds from the Father and the Son. All three *are not* one another.

This chapter will prove to be the longest in the book because the doctrine of the Trinity is the most difficult doctrine discussed in it. Even so, we have barely begun to explore the beauty of the Triune God. In fact, we could give the rest of our days to exploring the depth of glory that is in trinitarian theology, and we'd

12. William Shedd, *Dogmatic Theology* (P&R, 2003), 245. I first came across this quote in Sanders, *Triune God*, 128.

only realize that the further we press in, the more beauty there is to explore. However, it is time for us to turn from discussing a *definition* of the doctrine of the Trinity to *delighting* in it. Let us proceed to ask ourselves a vital question: How does the doctrine of the Trinity impact my daily life, and what would it look like to delight in a doctrine like God's being three in one?

Delighting in the Doctrine of the Trinity

Each chapter of this book ends with a section on how to delight in the doctrine discussed, and in some ways, delighting in the Trinity is both harder *and* easier than delighting in the other doctrines. It can feel harder to delight in the Trinity compared to other doctrines because of the *otherness* of God—the distinction between the One who creates and us, who are created. God is distinct and altogether different from us creatures, which can make the doctrine of the Trinity a difficult doctrine that feels somewhat abstract. Moreover, when we add doctrines that feel complex, like *homoousia* and eternal relations of origin, the whole thing can feel out of reach. While this posture is understandable, we should avoid thinking it is an impossible leap from God's triune nature to delight.

On the other hand, I can say that delighting in the Trinity is easier than delighting in other doctrines because it is not an exaggeration to say that the Trinity is the spring from which every other delight in this world flows. It is no overstatement to say that all things that are good, all things that are true, and all things that are beautiful exist only because of the Triune God and are grounded in the Triune God.

The Trinity as the Prize and Goal of the Christian Life

The Trinity is the wellspring of delight from which every lesser delight flows, and the doctrine of the Trinity ought to be one of the deepest and most visited wells of joy in our lives.

As fourth-century theologian Hilary of Poitiers writes, "Must not the Lord of this universal beauty be recognized as Himself most beautiful amid all the beauty that surrounds Him? For though the splendor of His eternal glory overtakes our mind's best powers, it cannot fail to see that He is beautiful."[13]

The first way we ought to properly delight in the Trinity is recognizing this Triune God as the goal of all things. You and I—and everything we have ever known—live, move, and have our being in God (Acts 17:28). Our lives and our very selves are from him, through him, and—an important point for the Christian life—one day going back *to* him (Rom. 11:36). At the end of all things, we get God. This is the supreme delight of the Christian life.

We await heaven and all the rewards therein. We eagerly long for the day when all sadness is unraveled at the seams; when endurance in the faith is a memory; when injustice takes its final breath as holy justice reigns; when we are remade and receive our glorified bodies. Yes, we long with great anticipation for all these things, yet what we want more than all these precious gifts is the Giver himself. The true prize of heaven is that, in the end, we get God. One day, we will be swallowed into his triune love in a way we cannot fathom this side of the resurrection. One day, King David's sole desire will be granted to you and me: "One thing have I asked of the Lord, that will I seek after: that I may dwell in the house of the Lord all the days of my life, to gaze upon the beauty of the Lord" (Ps. 27:4). We will one day receive our reward—seeing Christ face-to-face—and in that face our joy and delight will become complete beyond comprehension. Yes, we desire the gifts of heaven, but the deepest desire of our hearts is to be with the Triune God, who is the goal and reward of all things.

13. Hilary of Poitiers, "On the Trinity," in *Nicene and Post-Nicene Fathers Second Series*, vol. 1, ed. Philip Schaff and Henry Wace (Hendrickson, 2007), 7.

There are many application points flowing out of a biblical doctrine of the Trinity, more than we might imagine, but it is important to start with this point that may not *feel* applicational at all: The deepest delight of the Christian heart is God himself. The reason we can delight in the doctrine of the Trinity is because we believe *this* God is supremely worth knowing. With another psalmist, Asaph, Christians confess, "Whom have I in heaven but you? And *there is nothing on earth that I desire besides you.* My flesh and my heart may fail, but God is the strength of my heart and *my portion forever*" (Ps. 73:25–26). The Father, the Son, and the Holy Spirit are our portion forever. There is nothing on earth or in heaven we desire more than this Triune God. Without him we have nothing, and with him we have all we could dream of needing.

So, then, as we move on to other points of application and consider more ways we may delight in this particular doctrine, we keep this in mind: All delight comes from the hand of the Triune God.

The Trinity and Salvation

It does not take long for any study into the Christian doctrine of salvation to show just how trinitarian-shaped Christian salvation is. In fact, along with centuries of Christians who have come before us, we ought to confess that if we have no Trinity, we would have no salvation.

It could be said, in a basic way, that the Father plans salvation, the Son accomplishes salvation, and the Spirit applies salvation. This is true, to be certain, but we may do better in our articulation of the trinitarian shape of Christian salvation. While there are many places we could turn in Scripture to see this reality, the point is strikingly obvious in Paul's letter to the Galatians. He writes, "God has sent the Spirit of his Son into our hearts, crying, 'Abba! Father!' (Gal. 4:6). It is easy to read over, but do not miss the Trinity in this verse: "God [the first person] has sent the Spirit [the third person] of his Son [the second person] into our hearts."

In the fullness of time, God sends forth his Son to redeem a people whom the Father has chosen for himself before the foundation of the world. The Father gives these people to his Son. On their behalf, the Son is perfectly obedient to the law of the Father. The Spirit takes the righteousness of the Son and applies it to the people whom the Father has called out of the world. The Spirit unites these people to the Son so that they now obtain the merits of the Son, which allows them to stand before the Father and have communion with the Father, through the Son, by the Spirit. Throughout their lives, the Spirit continues to sanctify them into the image of the Son. After his ascension, the Son mediates on their behalf before the Father, interceding for them as their High Priest. As the Son was sent by the Father for his economic mission, the Father and the Son send the Spirit for his economic mission; in the mission of the Spirit, the third person will take all the Son has achieved and make it all theirs through their inheritance. In the meantime, the Spirit will be their seal and guarantee that this coming inheritance is really theirs. The final realization of this trinitarian salvation is that the people of this Triune God will get to behold the glory of the Trinity in the face of the Son as they eternally commune with the Father, the Son, and the Spirit in the life hereafter. Every step of our salvation—where we go from being sons and daughters of disobedience to being able to cry "Abba, Father"—is thoroughly trinitarian.

These are but a couple of the myriad ways Christians can spend their days delighting in the Trinity. This book will consider ten doctrines and will give substantial attention to asking how we may delight in each of them, but as mentioned before, each of the doctrines covered in this book—and every doctrine of the Christian faith—falls under the umbrella of the Trinity. All truth, all goodness, and all beauty flow from and participate in our Triune God. We then proclaim, with Augustine, that "this is the fullness of our joy, than which there is nothing greater: to enjoy God the Trinity in whose image we have been made."[14]

14. Augustine, *The Trinity* (CUA Press, 1963), 26.

2

Divine Attributes

Delighting in Perfection

To turn our mind's eye toward God's attributes is to set our sights on beauty upon beauty. Each one, like seeing a precious diamond from a new angle, gives us another view of God's perfection. Moreover, studying the divine attributes has the unique advantage of providing some illumination to all areas of theology. What I mean is this: Studying the divine attributes will impact what we think about nearly every other area of Christian theology, such as creation, salvation, the church, and more. When we give sustained attention to the divine attributes, the God who is the Author and Sustainer of all other areas of theology comes into view. We will know that creation was created by *this* God; that salvation is redemption by *this* God; that when we gather for worship, we are worshiping *this* God. Insomuch as lingering on them brings into focus who God is and what he is doing in the world, the divine attributes bring into focus *all* that is worthwhile.

Introducing the Doctrine of the Divine Attributes

There is often a feeling that comes with considering God's attributes, one of loftiness. It does not take long, when thinking about God's perfect essence, for the mind to be overwhelmed—and may it be so. If we understood all that it is to be God, it would no longer be God we are considering. His divine perfection will indeed flood the mind and the intellect with flashes of beauty beyond comprehension. Yet, I am convinced that if we can have the stability to stay the course and be the kind of undistracted people capable of sustained contemplation of God's being, it will transform the deepest places of our souls. Like how seeing something supremely beautiful leaves its mark on us, seeing the very One in whom beauty finds its origin will never leave us the same.

Theology is at its best when it is not read as a dry ledger of intellectual propositions but heard and seen as a symphony of beauty. Nowhere is the beauty of that symphony more pronounced than when we turn our mind's eye toward God himself. When we consider who God is—in the plenitude of his triune life—we are not only getting an eyeful of truth, beauty, and goodness, but also turning our gaze upon the One who is himself, in his very being, truth, beauty, and goodness—and the One from whom all lesser beauties flow.

We do not have the space here to cover all the divine attributes or to exhaust any one of them, for each attribute is an inexhaustible river of glory. Yet, my hope is to give enough time and consideration to God's attributes that readers will determine that this chapter simply is not enough and will use it as a springboard to jump deeper into the wonderful world of considering God's glory and grace through his attributes.

Defining the Doctrine of the Divine Attributes

Each of the divine attributes provides us another angle from which to view God's perfection. Each attribute is worth a full treatment of looking at all the Bible has to say about it, all the ways it shows God to be gloriously perfect, and all the ways it has significant import in the Christian life.

Defining Four Divine Attributes

I would like to do two things in this section: (1) cover a few selected attributes that readers may not be as familiar with, and (2) provide a brief chart and definition for many of the other attributes I was not able to cover in this chapter.

Choosing just a few attributes from the list the Bible gives us is like choosing which feast to join when all of them are delicious and nutritious for the soul. The four we will consider here have been chosen because they may be unfamiliar to some readers, since they have fallen out of favor in our modern evangelical imagination. Also, these four attributes allow us to discuss other glorious attributes along the way. They are divine incomprehensibility, divine simplicity, divine aseity, and divine immutability. If these doctrines sound unfamiliar to you at first read, you are not alone. Yet, each of these four attributes (like the others) offers a deep well of beauty Christians ought to revisit often.

1. Divine Incomprehensibility

At the beginning of all things, God kicked off the cosmos as we know it by a word. There was once nothing, then he spoke. As God spoke, *something* came from *nothing*. The opening salvo of Scripture tells us, "In the beginning, God created the heavens and the earth" (Gen. 1:1). In that act of making the heavens and the earth, beyond just creating the cosmos, God created a distinction—one many of us have never considered. When God spoke and all things came into being, there began a distinction that will remain forever. Now, after creation, everything that has ever existed falls into one of two categories: the Creator or the creature. There is One who spoke all things into being, and there are those who were *spoken into* being. There is One who called forth, and there are those who *were called* forth. There is One who has always existed, and there are those who *began* to exist.

This distinction is called the Creator-creature distinction, and it is one we will pick back up in chapter 4. However, I bring it up here to say that not only is there a distinction between he who created and those who were created, but there is also an impenetrable gap of knowledge between the two. The creatures cannot exhaustively know the Creator or wrap their minds around the Creator. The finite will never circumscribe the infinite. This leads us to a doctrine that has been affirmed across centuries and continents in the Christian church: the doctrine of divine incomprehensibility.

While there is much we could say about it, a working definition is this: The doctrine of divine incomprehensibility acknowledges the distinction between the Creator and the creature along with the implication that no creature will ever *fully* know God as he really is in his nature.[1] As we will see, this does not mean that we cannot *truly* know God; rather, it means that we cannot exhaust God with our finite minds and limited comprehension.

The notion of God being outside the comprehension of us mere creatures is a theme throughout the Scriptures. In Exodus 33, when Moses makes the audacious request to see the Lord's face, God informs him that "you cannot see my face, for man shall not see me and live" (v. 20). Elsewhere, the Scriptures say, "Even before a word is on my tongue, behold, O LORD, you know it altogether. You hem me in, behind and before, and lay your hand upon me. *Such knowledge is too wonderful for me; it*

1. I have written on this doctrine elsewhere and have given a more thorough definition, along with the needed nuances for more depth concerning God's incomprehensibility. See Ronni Kurtz, *Light Unapproachable: Divine Incomprehensibility and the Task of Theology* (IVP Academic, 2024).

is high; I cannot attain it" (Ps. 139:4–6), and "For my thoughts are not your thoughts, neither are your ways my ways, declares the LORD. For as the heavens are higher than the earth, so are my ways higher than your ways and my thoughts than your thoughts" (Isa. 55:8–9). We are told that God's "greatness is unsearchable" (Ps. 145:3) and that he "dwells in unapproachable light, whom no one has ever seen or can see" (1 Tim. 6:16).

However, while God indeed dwells in unapproachable light, he has nevertheless made himself known. God has *accommodated* himself such that he reveals himself in a way that we may not be able to *comprehend* but can *apprehend*—we cannot fully surround him with our minds, but our minds can grab hold of him. This means that due to God's gracious act of speaking to us in a way fitting for our creatureliness, we can meaningfully know God even if we cannot exhaustively know God.

2. Divine Simplicity

In its most basic form, the doctrine of divine simplicity teaches us that God is *not composed of parts*. In fact, there is *no* composition in God at all. God is not the sum of various ingredients that, when brought together in the right proportions—10 percent love, 20 percent justice, 15 percent holiness—voilà! His attributes—love, holiness, goodness, and the like—are not realities outside of God that combine to make God who he is, as this would make God dependent upon "parts" that are not God. God is not *dependent* on that which is not God. Rather, God *is* his attributes. This means God does not *have* love, as if love is a part of him that can wax and wane on any given day, like it does with us creatures. Instead, God *is* love. He does not *have* love; he *is* love (1 John 4:16). This is true for all God's attributes. God does not *have* attributes the way you and I have attributes. Rather, God *is* his essence.

Compare this idea to the way you and I are made up. We are remarkably complex creatures—not in terms of being difficult to understand but in terms of being composed of many different parts. From our attributes to our very bodies, we are a conglomeration. Not any one part of us *is us*. A rather silly example I often tell students is that if I were to lose a finger, I would remain Ronni. I might be less coordinated and have a few more hardships in holding items, but I would remain who I am without that finger. This is true because my essence and being are not defined by my fingers; in fact, my fingers—and much of my bodily parts—are expendable. I could lose a kidney or an arm and still be "me." Again, such losses would surely change some day-to-day activities, but these examples show that much of who I am is expendable. This expendability of my bodily anatomy and the changeableness of my emotional life show that I am a complex creature. Unlike God, I am composed of parts that come and go, parts that change, parts that are not identical to my essence.

God is not like this. There is nothing he could lose and remain who he is. For example, God cannot take off his holiness or remove his love. These do not wax and wane or come and go. These are not parts that make him up but his very existence. He does not *have* wisdom; he *is* wisdom. He does not *have* holiness, he *is* holy. An oft-repeated mantra about divine simplicity in church history is "All that is in God is God." This means God is not a composition of things that in themselves are not God—like love, holiness, wisdom, and so on. If he were, not only would God be dependent upon that which is not God, but he would also be in need of some outside composer who put the composition in order prior to God himself. Something would have to account for his composition, and this something would have to be greater than God. On the contrary, God himself is the great composer of all things and is in no need of an outside composer.

God's simplicity also guards against the idea of his attributes being in contradiction with one another. For example, it is not uncommon for Christians to, even unknowingly, pit God's love and God's justice against each other as if he must pick which one he is going to display at any particular time. Such as at the cross—is it a sign of God's love or his justice? Simplicity protects us from the error of choosing between these two and shows that God is love and justice in his very essence. He is not part love and part justice, part mercy and part truth. He is all that he is—all the time, all at once, in infinite perfection. This means there is never a moment when one of God's attributes is diminished or suspended. He does not turn off his justice to show love, nor must he balance his wrath against his mercy like weights on a scale. His entire being acts in harmony because he is perfectly unified in himself. When he acts in love, it is never less than holy. When he judges, it is never less than righteous and good. There are no parts of God to pit against one another. We as creatures may experience one attribute at a time, given our relationship to God at any given point, but this does not mean God is a complex being who is giving us an individual attribute at that particular time.

In Exodus 3:14, when God names himself for Moses, he tells the prophet, "I AM WHO I AM." God is himself; he is his essence. There is no distinction between God's essence and God's existence. He simply is. He is the One who is and who will be—forever himself, forever perfect, and forever gloriously the same. We will come back to the notion of divine simplicity in the delight section, for while this may seem like merely a philosophical idea, there are so many meaningful imports and implications for the Christian life from this vital doctrine.

3. Divine Aseity

We turn now to the doctrine of divine aseity, which is exceptional in its glory and beauty. In the simplest of terms, divine aseity means that God exists in and of himself. The word *aseity* comes from a Latin phrase—*a se*—which can mean "from oneself." There is both a positive and a negative way to think about divine aseity, and together they present a glorious truth about God's existence.[2] They are two sides of the same coin, two emphases that should not be pitted against each other, as they together create a robust understanding of the doctrine.

Negatively, God's aseity means that he depends on nothing and no one. There is nothing that gives God life, nothing that sustains God's life, and nothing that he depends on for life. Compare this to our existence: We are remarkably dependent creatures. If we do not have enough air, we perish; if we do not have enough food, we perish; if we are too cold or too hot, we perish. Moreover, we would not even have life had we not received it from our biological parents. The reality is, as offensive as it may sound, we are thoroughly dependent and shockingly fickle. In other words, we are not *a se*. We each live a derivative life, meaning our days depend on much that is outside our control.

The good news is that this is not the case with God. There is nothing that gives him life or sustains him. He is not dependent on parents, food, water, sustenance, shelter, or anything whatsoever. He needs no creator and he needs no sustainer; on the contrary, *he* is the Creator and Sustainer of all things.

However, the doctrine of divine aseity is more than a mere negative idea that God has no contingencies. In fact, divine aseity should also be considered a *positive* statement about God: He is the fullness of life in himself. The doctrine of aseity should be considered a trinitarian doctrine insomuch as the fullness of God's life is the product of the eternal relations among the persons. In the unbegotten Father, the eternally generated Son, and the Spirit who eternally proceeds from the Father and the Son, there is the fullness of life.

2. John Webster, *God Without Measure: Working Papers in Christian Theology*, God and the Works of God, vol. 1 (Bloomsbury T&T Clark, 2015), 13.

In the end, divine aseity is a rich attribute of God that ought to be the impetus for a lifetime of worship. As we will see, the implications for the Christian life springing from the doctrine of divine aseity are multifold.

4. Divine Immutability

In Malachi 3, the Lord says, "For I the LORD do not change" (v. 6). Likewise, in Numbers 23, we read, "God is not man, that he should lie, or a son of man, that he should change his mind" (v. 19). These two passages and many others like them describe a doctrine called divine immutability.

Francis Turretin, a seventeenth-century theologian, provides a short but helpful definition of divine immutability: "Immutability is an incommunicable attribute of God by which is denied of him not only all change, but also all possibility of change."[3] The doctrine of divine immutability helps put in perspective God's perfection. It should not surprise us to read that God is unchanging, for God is perfect. As many have pointed out throughout church history, if God were to change, his perfection would be in jeopardy. If God changes for the *better*, then he was not previously perfect; if God changes for the *worse*, then he is no longer perfect. Contrary to these two errors of thinking, God is unchanging and so, too, is his perfection. There is no need for activating change within God, for he is utterly perfect. His essence is perfect, his will is perfect, his attributes are perfect, his plans are perfect, his knowledge is perfect, his covenant faithfulness is perfect, his love is perfect. We can rejoice that our God is unchanging and, with Danish

3. Turretin, *Institutes of Elenctic Theology*, vol. 1, ed. James T. Dennison Jr., trans. George Musgrave Giger (P&R Publishing, 1992), 204. I have written on the doctrine of divine immutability at length elsewhere. See Ronni Kurtz, *No Shadow of Turning: Divine Immutability and the Economy of Redemption* (Christian Focus, 2022).

philosopher Søren Kierkegaard, confess, "In God's changelessness, there is rest."[4]

Not only does God's unchanging nature protect us from an ill-conceived understanding of perfection, but in God's changelessness is also the sturdy ground of our salvation. James roots God's graciousness in giving good gifts to his children in his unchanging nature, writing, "Every good gift and every perfect gift is from above, coming down from the Father of lights, with whom there is no variation or shadow due to change" (1:17). This is not a feature unique to James; a close and careful reading of Scripture shows that any assurance we have in our salvation is grounded in the fact that God is unchanging.

Moreover, insomuch as we can say—and as this chapter is at pains to say—that *any* of God's attributes are good news, they can really be good news only if they are unchanging. Consider this quote from seventeenth-century English theologian Stephen Charnock:

> Immutability is a glory belonging to all the attributes of God. . . . How cloudy would his blessedness be if it were changeable; how dim his wisdom if it might be obscured; how feeble his power if it were capable to be sickly and languish; how would mercy lose much of its lustre if it could change into wrath. . . . But unchangeableness is a thread that runs through the whole web. It is the enamel of all the rest.[5]

Charnock here is pointing out something profound: All of God's attributes are good news for Christians, and all of God's attributes are unchanging. It would be terrible news if God's goodness was as fickle and fleeting as our goodness. It would

4. Søren Kierkegaard, *The Moment and Late Writings*, ed. and trans. Howard Hong and Edna Hong (Princeton University Press, 1998), 278.

5. Stephen Charnock, *The Works of Stephen Charnock*, vol. 1 (Banner of Truth, 2010), 381.

be a travesty if his love could be thwarted or cut off in a fit of passion like so much creaturely love. The doctrine of divine immutability adds a stability to the Christian faith that is hard to find in our day. In a world where everything is fickle and fading, our God is ever the same.

Other Divine Attributes

Now that we have done the work of briefly defining the four attributes under consideration in this chapter, I want to at least mention a few others. While I wish space would permit a full observance of all these attributes and the beauty that flows from them, I simply want to end this section with a chart that gives a very basic definition of the attributes we have discussed and many we did not.

Divine Perfections

Name	Basic Definition
Simplicity	God is without parts.
Aseity	God has life in himself.
Plenitude	God's life is fullness, and he does not act out of lack.
Immutability	God does not change; it is impossible for God to change.
Impassability	God does not have passions.
Infinitude	God is not in any way measurable.
Eternality	God is not bound by time.
Omniscience	God is all-knowing.
Omnipresence	God is everywhere wholly present.
Omnisapience	God is all-wise.
Omnipotence	God is all-powerful.
Etc.	There are many other attributes of God.

Delighting in the Divine Attributes

The four attributes we considered above—incomprehensibility, simplicity, aseity, and immutability—are not merely truths to be affirmed in the mind; they are perfections meant to be savored with the heart. Theology, rightly understood, is never an end in itself; it is a pathway into praise. Few places is this truth more apparent than when considering the beauty of God's perfection. Therefore, the rest of this chapter will focus on delighting in these four attributes.

Delighting in Incomprehensibility

It may seem counterintuitive to consider how the doctrine of divine incomprehensibility can lead to delight in the Christian life. How could it possibly be good news that we cannot fully know God as he is? How can it be good news that, according to Exodus 33:20, if we see God's face, we will die? I will pick up more on this passage when we discuss the doctrine of accommodation in chapter 4. However, we should start this section with an easy to miss fact: A god you could fully comprehend would not be worthy of worship. In a letter to her friend, novelist and essayist Flannery O'Connor once wrote, "Whatever you do anyway, remember that these things are mysteries and that if they were such that we could understand them, they wouldn't be worth understanding. *A God you understood would be less than yourself.*"[6]

Far be it from us to want a comprehensible god who is easily boxed up and packaged within an intellectual system. Rather, we worship the God who breathed out the stars and told the oceans their boundaries. As John says, if the works of Christ—during his incarnation alone—were all written down, "I suppose that the world itself could not contain the books that would be written" (John 21:25).

There are many avenues to follow when tracing the beauty of incomprehensibility; among my favorite to consider is that

6. Flannery O'Connor, *The Habit of Being: Letters of Flannery O'Connor* (Noonday Press, 1979), 345, emphasis added.

God's incomprehensibility means that whatever stirs our affections for the Lord—*that very thing* is without end. Maybe it is God's love that most demonstrates his majesty before your mind's eye; maybe God's holiness is the attribute that most commands your affection's attention; maybe God's sovereignty and providence most cause awe as you stand before him. Whatever it is, whatever about our great God kicks up that fire in your stomach and causes your soul to ache with desire to see and be near him—it is endless. You could spend the rest of your days exploring God's love; it is incomprehensibly deep, so keep going. You will never reach the bottom. Spend a thousand lifetimes traversing his glory, and you will be no closer to exhausting it than you were when you began. God will always be greater than your best thought of him, more glorious than your best word about him, and deeper than your most profound contemplation of him.

The doctrine of divine incomprehensibility should be the death of the idea that heaven may be boring. Instead, incomprehensibility is the very doctrine that gives meaning and beauty to C. S. Lewis's magnificent heavenly phrase: "further up and further in."[7]

Heaven will be the world where we can—*forever*—keep pressing into God's glory. Given that incomprehensibility is predicated on the Creator-creature distinction and that this distinction will not be rendered untrue in heaven, even in heaven God will be incomprehensible—and this is terrifically good news. In heaven, we will have eyes to see him that we do not yet possess; we will have a vision of him we could not dare even dream in this life. Even with the beatific vision and glorified eyes and mind, we *still* will not plumb his depths. Heaven, then, will truly be a continual *further up* and *further in*—we

7. C. S. Lewis, *The Last Battle* (HarperCollins, 1984), 196. © copyright 1956 CS Lewis Pte Ltd. All extracts used by permission.

will increasingly apprehend his beauty but will never exhaust his beauty as to comprehend him. It will be as the song says: "When we've been there ten thousand years, bright shining as the sun, we've no less days to sing God's praise than when we first begun."[8]

Delighting in Simplicity

Of the four doctrines we discussed in this chapter—incomprehensibility, simplicity, aseity, and immutability—the doctrine of divine simplicity is most likely the one that ordinary Christians have heard the least about. It is also the one that many in our modern era may have the hardest time accepting. One complaint against the doctrine of divine simplicity—that God is not composed of parts—is that it is too abstract, or, to use a more technical word, it is too *metaphysical*. Some think it is too reliant on philosophy and is not stated clearly enough in any one biblical passage to be a doctrine of importance. While I do not intend to defend the doctrine against its detractors here, I do want to spend a little bit of time working against the idea that the doctrine of divine simplicity is too abstract to be of any use for Christian faith and life. I am convinced that while it may *sound* like an abstract doctrine—and in some ways it is abstract—there is nevertheless profound beauty in this doctrine just as there is profound beauty in all of God's perfections.

When it comes to explaining the *wonder* that is the doctrine of divine simplicity, I like to use two ideas of glory: the glory of where we come from and the glory of where we are going. These two notions of God's glory are tied up in the doctrine of simplicity in profoundly beautiful ways.

First, "the glory of where we come from" brings us back to the idea of composition. The doctrine of divine simplicity says that God is not composed of parts—not the sum of various

8. "Amazing Grace," lyrics by John Newton (1779). Public domain.

parts that, put together the right way, give him life. God has no parts and therefore needs no composition. That word, *composition*, is quite important when trying to understand divine simplicity. Think of a child playing with LEGOs. At first, there is a large bag of LEGOs of all shapes and sizes. Let's say the child dumps the bag on the ground and begins creating a great castle. The LEGOs are separate parts—smaller units than the whole that is being built—and come in all shapes, sizes, and colors. If you were to pick up one LEGO and say, "Look, a castle!" you'd be mistaken; that LEGO may well be *part* of what makes up the castle, but itself is not a castle.

If the LEGOs were just left on the floor as individual parts, they would never form a castle. To become a castle, the LEGOs need a *composer*—someone to give them order and purpose; they need someone to take the individual parts and make them a collective whole. This is true of *any* composition. Everything that has been composed needs a composer: music, art, nature, construction, physics, engineering, and so on. If you were at a symphony and all the musicians played whatever they felt like playing at the same time, it would be not a symphony but a cacophony. The sound would be one not of beauty and harmony but of disorder and chaos. Or, if you were at a construction site and all the builders built as they pleased, they would likely produce not something lasting and beautiful but something uninhabitable and ugly. All things, creation included, need a composer in order to bring harmony and beauty out of chaos and noise.

Yet, only one greater than what is being composed can bring such composition. A child can bring composition to the LEGOs, but someone must also give composition to that child. As odd as it may sound, the child—like the LEGOs—is a complex system of various parts, a conglomeration of muscles and nerves, of fingers and toes, of brain and heart. Not any one of those anatomical parts is a child in itself, but together they come together to make a child. This reveals so much beauty in a verse like "For you formed my inward parts; you knitted me together in my mother's womb. I praise you, for I am fearfully and wonderfully made. Wonderful are your works; my soul knows it very well" (Ps. 139:13–14).

God is uniquely qualified to compose each one of us and bring harmony out of the variegated parts that make us who we are. However, he does not stop with each child personally knit together in each mother's womb. God's composing work extends to all the cosmos. God, as the only One who is *simple*, is the only One capable of giving composition to creation. All complex creatures—that is, those composed of individual parts—need a composer. We need a noncomplex being to begin the glorious composing work. In God, we have just that noncomplex being. The simple One. The One who is the great I Am—*I am who I am*—is the simple One who brings glorious harmony to the cosmos. When we look around at his beautiful creation, we see order, rhythm, and harmony. Very complex features like nature and life, animals and humans, seas and tides, planets and stars, all of it—individual pieces as they are—are brought together in a harmonious composition that declares the glory of the simple One who brings harmony to chaos (Ps. 19:1).

For the second glory—"the glory of where we are going"—simplicity has another staggering encouragement to offer us believers. I am a person deeply motivated by the true, the good, and the beautiful. These three together are often called "the transcendental." Every night I pray over my children that they will grow to be the kind of people who can apprehend what is true in the world, what is good in creation, and what is beautiful in our cosmos. I pray that in a noisy world, where a million lesser loves call for their attention, their souls will be cultivated enough to keep their minds on these things. How does the transcendental of the true, the good, and the beautiful relate to divine simplicity? Because God is simple and does not *have* truth, does not *have* goodness, and does not *have* beauty but *is* truth, goodness, and beauty in himself, pursuing these three things is not three separate journeys. Truth, beauty, and goodness are all grounded in the same source: God himself. He is truth, he is goodness, he is the very definition of that which is beautiful. If God answers my prayer to give my children these three things, he will do so by giving them *himself*.

In fact, whatever good you desire in your life, it is grounded in God. Your pursuit of justice, of holiness, of beauty, of goodness, of righteousness, of meaning—it is all, or at least it should be, a pursuit of God in himself. It is why Paul can tell the Philippian church, "Finally, brothers and sisters, whatever is true, whatever is noble, whatever is right, whatever is pure, whatever is lovely, whatever is admirable—if anything is excellent or praiseworthy—think about such things" (Phil. 4:8 NIV). All excellent or praiseworthy things find their value in participating in the excellent and praiseworthy God who makes all these pursuits one—a pursuit of him.

So, simplicity gives us a glory of where we have come from—a gloriously simple composer who brings harmony. And simplicity also shows us a glory of where we are going—a gloriously simple God who is himself all that is excellent and praiseworthy.

Delighting in Aseity

God does not need you or me.

At first glance, this may strike us as offensive or somehow bad news. Yet, it is a profoundly freeing and beautiful thought, which aseity gives us the foundation to have.

God is the fullness of life in himself. There is nothing he needs that would bring him greater fulfillment. There is nothing missing in him that must be supplied. God has no potential that needs to be actualized or awakened. He is supremely perfect in the plenitude of his own life. This means you and

I do not meet a need God has been longing for; we do not satisfy a craving he has or fill a hole in his life. The God who has the cattle on a thousand hills does not need you and me. As he himself says:

> For every beast of the forest is mine,
> the cattle on a thousand hills.
> I know all the birds of the hills,
> and all that moves in the field is mine.
>
> "If I were hungry, I would not tell you,
> for the world and its fullness are mine." (Ps. 50:10–12)

A similar theme comes from the prophet Isaiah, who, through rhetorical questions, shows that we cannot supply God with anything he does not have or complete anything for him:

> Who has measured the Spirit of the LORD,
> or what man shows him his counsel?
> Whom did he consult,
> and who made him understand?
> Who taught him the path of justice,
> and taught him knowledge,
> and showed him the way of understanding? (Isa. 40:13–14)

Paul asks the Corinthian church, "What do you have that you did not receive?" (1 Cor. 4:7), and we could reverse the question: "What could we give God that he does not already own?" Or, as Luke writes, "The God who made the world and everything in it, being Lord of heaven and earth, does not live in temples made by man, *nor is he served by human hands, as though he needed anything*, since he himself gives to all mankind life and breath and everything" (Acts 17:24–25).

These passages come together to make it quite clear: God is not in need of us. The beauty in this statement is hard to put into words. Yet, it shines through when we ask an important question in light of what we have said so far: Why does God do anything God does? For example, why did God create? Why did God save you and me?

We know from these passages that God did not create due to lack or loneliness. The trillions of stars in the sky and the billions of inhabitants on earth do not give God something he was missing. Here is where the beauty of divine aseity rushes in: God acts not out of lack but out of plenitude. From creation, to redemption, to consummation, to providence, God does all he does out of the abundance of his own life.

Salvation is a wonderful example: God did not save you because of *you*. He was not looking down from his throne room and, after enough pity welled up within him, decided it was time to regenerate your soul and bring you into saving faith. Nor was it the case that by some valiant effort of righteousness you caught God's eye and, out of sheer impressiveness on your part, he was moved to deliver you from the domain of darkness. No; God saves not because of some high or low in your life but out of the plenitude of his *own life*. He creates out of plenitude; he saves out of plenitude; he loves out of plenitude. The One who is *a se*—of himself—points his plenitude in our direction, and the results are unspeakable joys and unfathomable riches of grace.

The beauty in this is striking and may just be the grace-laced dagger needed to pierce your heart. *Nothing* in you moves God to do what God does. God does what he does because he is who he is. He operates out of the fullness of his being.

Delighting in Immutability

The doctrine of divine immutability holds a special importance for me. Yes, I wrote my doctoral dissertation on the doctrine of divine immutability. But, more importantly, I wrote that dissertation between 2018 and 2021, years that proved to be a period of significant change for my wife and me. During those years, my mother passed away from cardiac arrest, we had our first child, I took my first professor position—not to mention that COVID-19 shook things up across the globe, causing much change in the church I pastored and disrupting many other life rhythms.

With so much change, both joyous and painful, happening during those years, the doctrine of God's changelessness became not just something to be examined for a doctoral dissertation but a perfection of God that led me to exaltation. When the world around us feels unstable and ever in flux, there is a comfort for the soul in knowing that our Triune God is ever the same.

As I spent those years steeped in Scripture and other writings about God's unchanging nature, one emphasis about God's changelessness began to jump out at me as particularly comforting. When the Scriptures bring up the idea of the Lord being unchanging, it is often in the context of his work in saving a wayward people. Malachi 3:6, the passage that seems to most directly indicate that God is immutable, mentions not just that God is unchanging but that his unchanging nature is good news for his people and their salvation. The verse starts off with an explicit affirmation of divine immutability: "For I the Lord do not change." Then the text goes on to state the implication of God's immutability: "Therefore you, O children of Jacob, are not consumed."

In another example, from the book of Numbers, Balaam says, "God is not man, that he should lie, or a son of man, that he should change his mind," a confident assurance of God's immutability that leads Balaam to reassure his hearers, "Has he said, and will he not do it? Or has he spoken, and will he not fulfill it?" (23:19). God, speaking through Balaam, is reminding his people that he is unchanging and does not change his mind—therefore, if he has said he will do something, he will do it. He is not double-minded like humans who may promise one thing and betray their word. On the contrary, the immutable God will always keep his covenant promises.

It should not surprise us that salvation is often in view when the Scriptures discuss God's immutability, for it is on the foundation of God's unchanging nature that we can have assurance of our salvation. To make it plain, consider the ways God's unchanging nature—like many ropes that hold a ship to the dock—creates a bond of assurance untouchable by this world.

God the Father, the unchanging first person of the Trinity, has immutably elected us for salvation, and "has he said, and will he not do it? Or has he spoken, and will he not fulfill it?" (Num. 23:19). This immutable election from before the foundation of the world is based not on our action or participation but on his immutable will and immutable glory. God the Son, the unchanging second person of the Trinity, has taken on flesh and secured an immutable righteousness through his perfect obedience to the law. After his death, burial, resurrection, and then ascension to the right hand of the Father, he now, because he is not prevented by death like the former high priests (Heb. 7:22–28), can ever live to make immutable intercession for us that is able to immutably save us to the uttermost. Moreover, God the Spirit, the unchanging third person of the Trinity, takes the immutable righteousness of the Son and through immutably uniting us to that very Son makes that immutable righteousness immutably ours. The Holy Spirit himself is the immutable seal and guarantee that this immutable salvation will be brought to completion on the day of judgment. After which, we will enjoy an immutable eternity, ever living in immutable righteousness, gazing at and worshiping the immutable Triune God.

Flowing from the beautiful well of divine immutability is glory and grace that ought to be the impetus for a lifetime of praise. I will bring this section to a close with the prince of preachers—Charles Haddon Spurgeon—delighting in the good news that is our unchanging God:

> Remember God is the same, whatever is removed. Your friends may be disaffected, your ministers may be taken away, everything may change, but God does not. Your brethren may change and cast out your name as vile: but God will love you still. Let your station in life change, and your property be gone; let your whole life be shaken, and you become weak and sickly; let everything flee away—there is one place where change cannot put his finger; there is one name on which mutability can never be written; there is one heart which never can alter; that heart is God's—that name Love.[9]

Delighting in God's Attributes

We have, of course, touched on the glory and beauty of only four attributes of God; there are many more. We have said nothing of how God's omnipresence puts any loneliness we feel to flight. We have not discussed how God's omniscience means that the One who knows us most thoroughly loves us most fully. We have not discussed how divine impassability renders God capable to do something about suffering, and how he does not need to be *moved* to love us. Each divine perfection is an incomprehensibly deep ocean of truth, beauty, and goodness we could spend the rest of our days swimming in—and we would never find the shore on the other side. It is no wonder that biblical benedictions and salutations—the writers' goodbyes and hellos—often simply beckon us to glorify this great God. So, with the apostles, we say, "To [God] be the glory forever and ever. Amen" (Gal. 1:5).

9. Charles H. Spurgeon, "The Immutability of God," in *New Park Street Pulpit*, vol. 1 (Passmore & Alabaster, 1855), 8.

3

Creation

Delighting in Your Maker

I have an affinity for C. S. Lewis's depiction of creation in his masterpiece of a children's series, The Chronicles of Narnia. My students are used to me using Lewis's creation scene often in teaching the doctrine at the undergraduate level. It takes place in *The Magician's Nephew*, and there is much Lewis gets right about the doctrine of creation that is easy to miss. To set the scene: A handful of characters find themselves in an uninhabited world filled with nothingness. In time, this nothingness is pierced with a sound that is eventually recognized as a majestic song:

> In the darkness something was happening at last. A voice had begun to sing. It was very far away and Digory found it hard to decide from what direction it was coming. Sometimes it seemed to come from all directions at once. Sometimes he almost thought it was coming out of the earth beneath them. Its lower notes were deep enough to be the voice of the earth

> herself. There were no words. There was hardly even a tune. But it was, beyond comparison, the most beautiful noise he had ever heard. It was so beautiful he could hardly bear it. . . . Then two wonders happened at the same moment. One was that the voice was suddenly joined by other voices; more voices than you could possibly count. They were in harmony with it, but far higher up the scale: cold, tingling, silvery voices. The second wonder was that the blackness overhead, all at once, was blazing with stars. They didn't come out gently one by one, as they do on a summer evening. One moment there had been nothing but darkness; next moment a thousand, thousand points of light leaped out—single stars, constellations, and planets, brighter and bigger than any in our world.[1]

Readers familiar with the story will know that what Digory hears is the song of Aslan the Lion, who is singing Narnia into existence. There is something *right* and *beautiful* about explaining creation as a song. In fact, we know that the heavens themselves "declare the glory of God" (Ps. 19:1) and that "the morning stars sang together" the song of creation (Job 38:7). There would be much gladness to be had if we could tune our souls to the frequency of the cosmos's song. This is a theme we will return to in the delight section of this chapter, but for now I'll just remind you, as I often like to remind my students after I read them this beautiful scene from Narnia, that it pales in comparison to the beauty that is the real creation of the cosmos.

Introducing the Doctrine of Creation

The true song of God—his speaking something out of nothing—is beautiful beyond our comprehension. While the full

1. C. S. Lewis, *The Magician's Nephew* (HarperCollins, 1983), 106–7. © copyright 1955 CS Lewis Pte Ltd. All extracts used by permission.

beauty of God's creation is outside our ability to comprehend, we get a glimpse of it in Job 38. This scene comes after a long back-and-forth between Job and his friends as to the cause and nature of his suffering. When God shows up to answer Job and respond to his friends' questioning of God, it is among the most jaw-dropping portions of Scripture we have in our Bibles. God answers Job—but he answers with a long list of questions that can be summarized as "Where were you when I brought forth the cosmos out of nothing?" This section starts with a passage that should leave a lump in our throats: "Then the Lord answered Job out of the whirlwind and said: 'Who is this that darkens counsel by words without knowledge? Dress for action like a man; I will question you, and you make it known to me'" (Job 38:1–3).

God beckons Job to "dress for action" and instructs the suffering man to answer for his grievances and complaints against God's providence (Job 38:3). While the scene lasts longer than one chapter, and these are not *all* the questions God puts before Job, Job 38 gives us a glimpse of just how majestic God's work of creation is. Though we could never properly know what it would be like to participate in these actions, we can consider just how beautiful God's speaking something out of nothing really is. As you read God's questions, allow your mind's eye to imagine the splendor of the words and the beauty of the realities they describe.

> Where were you when I laid the foundation of the earth? (v. 4)
>
> Who determined its measurements? (v. 5)
>
> On what were its bases sunk, or who laid its cornerstone? (v. 6)
>
> [Where were you] when the morning stars sang together and all the sons of God shouted for joy? (v. 7)

Who shut in the sea with doors when it burst out from the womb? (v. 8)

Have you commanded the morning since your days began, and caused the dawn to know its place? (v. 12)

Have you entered into the springs of the sea, or walked in the recesses of the deep? (v. 16)

Have you comprehended the expanse of the earth? (v. 18)

Where is the way to the dwelling of light, and where is the place of darkness? (v. 19)

What is the way to the place where the light is distributed, or where the east wind is scattered upon the earth? (v. 24)

Who has cleft a channel for the torrents of rain and a way for the thunderbolt? (v. 25)

Has the rain a father, or who has begotten the drops of dew? (v. 28)

From whose womb did the ice come forth, and who has given birth to the frost of heaven? (v. 29)

Can you bind the chains of the Pleiades or loose the cords of Orion? (v. 31)

Do you know the ordinances of the heavens? Can you establish their rule on the earth? (v. 33)

Can you lift up your voice to the clouds, that a flood of waters may cover you? (v. 34)

Can you send forth lightnings, that they may go and say to you, "Here we are"? (v. 35)

Who can number the clouds by wisdom? (v. 37)

Can you hunt the prey for the lion? (v. 39)

Who provides for the raven its prey? (v. 41)

This brutal line of questioning was sure to make Job feel microscopically small (and it goes on for two full chapters more).

At the end of God's interrogation, Job rightly responds with profound humility as he admits the mistake of any creature putting the Creator to questioning. With trembling and humility, Job responds, "I have uttered what I did not understand, things too wonderful for me, which I did not know. . . . I had heard of you by the hearing of the ear, but now my eye sees you; therefore I despise myself, and repent in dust and ashes" (Job 42:3, 5–6).

So, then, we proceed—hoping to define and delight in the doctrine of creation, but we ought to do so with the trembling and humility of Job. When speaking about creation and God's majestic work, we ensure the question he put before Job never leaves our minds: *Where were you?* This is the correct theological posture for contemplating creation, and it will be the one needed to allow the doctrine of creation to have its proper effect on us: to remind us, with Job, of our smallness; to help us live stable lives in tune with creation; and to allow creation to stir us on to greater faithfulness. Before we can get to these meaningful application points, however, we need to develop a theology of creation.

Defining the Doctrine of Creation

This chapter marks a turn in the doctrines we are considering. The first two—the doctrine of the Trinity and the doctrine of God's attributes—are what we call "theology proper," meaning they are about God as he is without reference to anyone else. For example, if God never created the world, he would still be immutable, or unchanging. If God never saved humanity, he would still be triune. Theology proper deals with who God is. However, this great God we have been considering for two chapters has also turned outward, toward us. In line with this, we could say theology focuses on two things: God's internal life and his external life. In theology, you may hear these two topics referred to as the *ad intra* and the *ad extra*. Do not be intimidated by these Latin phrases; they are simply ways to describe what we have already been talking about. The phrase *ad intra*, in its most basic form, means "internal," while *ad extra* means "external."

	Ad Intra	Ad Extra
Definition	The first subject of theology: God himself Theology that deals with God as he is in himself without reference to creation or creatures	The second subject of theology: all things in relation to God Theology that deals with God's actions externally as God acts toward creation and creatures
Doctrinal Examples	The doctrine of the Trinity Divine attributes Eternal relations of origin God's being and essence	Creation Salvation Providence Incarnation
Direction and Emphasis	Internal—God's own life Theology proper	External—God's actions Economy

The reason the distinction between *ad intra* and *ad extra* is important to bring up at this point is that the doctrine of creation is the first we are considering that is an act of God *ad extra*—or external to himself. As we consider creation, we are no longer considering God as he is; rather, we are considering an act he has done toward his creatures—namely, bringing them into existence. In fact, everything we will talk about from this point on is part of God's "economy," or his outward action—the *ad extra*. From creating us, to saving us, to gathering us up in what we call the church, to eventually coming back and completing the salvation on behalf of us.

As we turn to that preeminent work in God's economy—the creation of all things—I want to bring our focus toward two doctrines that will help us establish a robust view of creation: (1) the doctrine of creation *ex nihilo* ("out of nothing") and (2) the doctrine of the Creator-creature distinction. While these two doctrines alone are far from the only doctrines to explore in understanding creation, they are significant and have a wide enough range that, in considering them, much of the beauty of creation should come into our view.

Creation Ex Nihilo

Fairly steady in the history of God's people has been an affirmation of the doctrine called creation *ex nihilo*. This Latin phrase simply means "out of nothing." It negates any notion of preexistent matter and proclaims that God is not merely a craftsman who shapes and sculpts material that always existed but truly a *Creator* who brought something where there was once nothing. The Christian doctrine of creation *ex nihilo* constitutes a profound confession about all matter and reality: God, without constraint or compulsion, brought all things into existence where previously there was nothing—not even the potential for something. It stands in sharp contrast to ancient stories of the origin of the cosmos, which often depict divine beings ordering chaotic material, and it resists modern philosophical accounts that interpret creation as either an emanation from God or the result of some impersonal processes. Rather, the Christian vision insists that creation begins in God's free and intentional speech, not from necessity or lack.

Moreover, creation *ex nihilo* reminds us that whatever we say about our doctrine of creation, it must remain God-centered. As John Webster once said, "The starting point for a Christian doctrine of creation, as for any Christian doctrine, is God in himself. . . . Only out of the sheer antecedent perfection of God's life *in se* can we feel the force of the concept of creation."[2] Webster is correct here. A doctrine of creation is only as good as the doctrine of God that undergirds and animates it. Consider

2. John Webster, *God Without Measure: Working Papers in Christian Theology*, God and the Works of God, vol. 1 (T&T Clark, 2015), 88.

how Scripture begins in the first place: "In the beginning, God created" (Gen 1:1). Even in this opening salvo of Holy Scripture we can see the proper order of a doctrine of creation: in the beginning (1) God, (2) created. God is the primary actor in the wonder that is creation's coming into existence. Matter is not some sort of divine LEGO set already there before the foundations of the world with which God sculpted the world. The fundamental confession of creation *ex nihilo* is this: There was once only God living, and out of his fullness he spoke—and nothing gave way to something.

There is a difficulty to understanding creation *ex nihilo* not only because it is impossible to wrap our minds around what it means for God to create but also because it is hard to wrap our minds around the notion of "nothing." Catholic theologian Michael Dodds makes this very point in an accessible way:

> It should come as no surprise that the act of creation—the production of something from nothing—is very mysterious. If you've ever tried to think of nothing, you've probably failed and ended up thinking of something—such as an empty space, or darkness, or even the very word n-o-t-h-i-n-g.[3]

This quote is helpful in showing the sheer *otherness* of God. Only the One who has the power of life in himself, as Scripture says in John 5:26, could have the kind of power needed to bring life where there was no life. It would be marvelous enough if God crafted the world and brought the complex beauty that is our cosmos out of some preexistent material. It is a whole other depth of profound mystery and beauty to say that, instead, where there was nothing—a concept we have trouble considering in itself—God spoke everything.

3. Michael Dodds, *The One Creator God in Thomas Aquinas and Contemporary Theology* (CUA, 2020), 159.

We will pursue this more in the delight section, but there is beauty to be found in the doctrine of creation *ex nihilo*. It emerges not only as a metaphysical commitment (something we believe) but also as a doxological declaration (something we proclaim). Creation *ex nihilo* ought to humble the creature and magnify the Creator as it frames the world as the theater of divine generosity. It renders every act of existence a gift and every moment of history an unfolding of divine intention. And it reminds the church that just as the world began in grace, so it shall culminate in glory.

Creator-Creature Distinction

One of the most significant implications of creation's being out of nothing is the distinction the doctrine puts between he who created and those who were created. If creation *ex nihilo* is true, then we can think of a time when all matter that has ever existed outside of God himself did not exist. It all *came* into being and therefore is in the process of *becoming*, and it has its being only because God has spoken it to be so. Unlike God, who is forever unchanging and is not *becoming* but *being* itself, creation is in constant motion, moving toward what it was meant to be. This means there is a sharp contrast between God and all other things. We can, rightly, place all that has ever existed and all that will exist in one of two categories: God and *not* God.

This distinction in theology is called the Creator-creature distinction. The distinction between the Creator and those who were created has received much attention throughout church history, and for good reason. Getting this correct is the protection the church needs to save her from idolatry. It seems that Paul even has something like this distinction in mind when he writes to the Romans, "They exchanged the truth about God for a lie and worshiped and served the *creature* rather than the *Creator*, who is blessed forever! Amen" (1:25). Paul is writing against those who "exchanged the glory of the immortal God for images resembling mortal man and birds and animals and creeping things" (1:23). In the place of the immortal being who has always existed and who spoke all into being, these people—who, though foolish, claimed to be wise—put lesser loves. They put in the place of the Creator that which is created or even images of that which has been created.

When the Creator-creature distinction comes into play, it ought to humble the creature and show the Creator to be the majestic maker he is. This is why theologians have made the distinction such an emphasis in their thinking and writing. Listen to Herman Bavinck describe the profound gulf that exists between the Creator and creation:

> The distance between God and us is the gulf between the Infinite and the finite, between eternity and time, between being and becoming, between the All and the nothing. However little we know of God, even the faintest notion implies that he is a being who is infinitely exalted above every creature.[4]

Notice the comparisons Bavinck gives us here: infinite versus finite, being versus becoming. These distinctions are far from superficial; they show a God who is completely *other* than his creation.

An important point to make regarding the Creator-creature distinction is that God is not quantifiable or measurable. God is not distinct from his creation because he is merely bigger or grander. To put it another way, God is not just an infinitely bigger version of the creature. Rather, the Creator-creature distinction is one of *kind*. While we are created in his image and designed to reflect his creative power, there is still, from our perspective, an untraversable gulf between God and not

4. Herman Bavinck, *Reformed Dogmatics*, vol. 2, ed. John Bolt (Baker Academic, 2004), 30.

God. This gulf is where we turn toward delight, which rushes into our consideration of God's creative act.

Delighting in the Doctrine of Creation

The Creator-creature distinction is a great place to segue into our section on delighting in the doctrine of creation. To begin, it puts into perspective the scandal and wonder that is the incarnation of Jesus Christ.

Creation and the Wonder of the Incarnation

The gulf between the Creator and the created is insurmountable for us creatures. We could have infinite generations come and go, and we would be no closer to clawing or crawling our way to divinity than we are now. Yet, the gospel of Christ speaks a better word, one in which the divine traverses the uncrossable gulf to us. In our deepest need, Christ—the One through whom and for whom all things were created—takes on flesh and dwells among us creatures. Then, in Christian salvation, by faith, the Holy Spirit unites us to Christ that we may be resurrected and ascend with him to enjoy the presence of God our Creator in perfect harmony and glory for all eternity.

There is a near unspeakable wonder in the union of the Creator and the creature in the person of Christ—divinity and humanity united in order to redeem an unworthy people. It is easy to confess that the incarnation is profound, but bringing the Creator-creature distinction into the conversation gives some categories to this profundity. It is only when we see just how different the Creator and the creatures really are in their being that we can begin to appreciate the wonder that is the Creator assuming the flesh of the creatures. The gulf between the Creator and the creature will never go away—even in eternity, when we will have a glorified existence, we will yet be glorified *creatures*. When we arrive on that great golden shore, by grace we will get to participate in what God is by nature. Yet, even in our everlasting participation in God, we will ever remain creatures. However, we can still confess, with the history of the church, this great reality: "The Son of God became a man to enable men to become sons of God."[5]

The Good News of Creatureliness

It is an obvious point, but one too vital to simply pass over: We are creatures. We are numbered among those who were spoken into being. If it is true that everything that has ever existed can be divided into two categories—that which is God and that which is *not God*—then you and I belong squarely in the latter category. You are not God. I am not God. We are limited creatures, and there is a sweet freedom that comes from pressing in to the confines of our limitedness. Every day, our stomachs send us hunger signals; as we age, our muscles and joints begin to ache; each night, our eyelids get heavy with sleep. While these limitations can carry with them immense frustrations, they, and many like them, are daily reminders that we are creatures whose days are numbered. Wisdom is not trying to outwit our creatureliness and escape our embodied limitations but pressing in to God's good design and allowing the very limitations of finitude we protest to teach us a true and better word about the gospel and glory of the limitless, infinite Creator of the cosmos.

It is not just our days that are numbered. Our output is numbered, our production is numbered, our energy is numbered, and our love is numbered. We are numbered creatures. Though we live in an age that consistently catechizes us to hate being limited, what we see in Scripture is the opposite notion: "A heart of wisdom" comes from asking the Lord to "*teach* us to number our days" (Ps. 90:12).

5. C. S. Lewis, *Mere Christianity* (HarperCollins, 1980), 178. © copyright 1942, 1943, 1944, 1952 CS Lewis Pte Ltd. All extracts used by permission.

If we are to have cultivated souls and be people of wisdom and stability, it is vital we recognize the beauty of the biblical reality that dependence is *not* a consequence of the fall. On the contrary, Adam and Eve were dependent on God as part of God's good design. It is only *after* the fall, as sin took root in the heart of humanity, that we sought to establish our own *in*dependence. Creatureliness and the dependence found in our being creatures are a gift from God, who alone is the plenitude of life and needs no other. As Kelly Kapic says in his wonderful treatment of human finitude and creatureliness, *You're Only Human*:

> We must rediscover that being *dependent* creatures is a constructive gift, not a deficiency. Clever readers might even notice that using "dependent" as an adjective for "creature" is basically redundant—there are no creatures who are not, by their very nature, dependent beings. Our dependency does not merely point to abstract ideas of divine providence, but takes concrete form when we rely on others, on the earth, on institutions, and traditions. We must learn the value and truthfulness of our finitude, eventually getting to the point where *we might even praise God for our limits*.[6]

Tuning Our Souls to the Cosmos's Song

One of the beauties about the doctrine of creation is that it gets at the very things that make us human. Creation reminds us that by his grace God took that which is ordinary and mundane—the dust of the earth—and breathed life into it. At our very core, we are dependent creatures. Just as we were dependent upon God to breathe life into the dust, we are dependent upon him for every breath we have taken and will ever take.

6. Kelly Kapic, *You're Only Human: How Your Limits Reflect God's Design and Why That's Good News* (Brazos, 2022), 10–11.

Beyond merely reminding us of our dependence on God, however, a mature doctrine of creation can also help explain our *longings*. In his book about Ecclesiastes, *Everything Is Never Enough*, Bobby Jamieson utilizes the work of Hartmut Rosa to discuss a notion called *resonance*. Jamieson explains, "Resonance occurs when some aspect of the world moves you, reaches you, touches you, or calls to you. In resonance, the wire connecting you to the world starts to hum."[7] To put it simply: This is the feeling when the happenings of the world resonate within us and, even for a moment, we feel like the world makes sense, and we have that profound sense of meaning and beauty.

This notion of resonance with the earth is one of the reasons I love that C. S. Lewis uses the concept of music and song to show Aslan creating Narnia. It bodes well with the passage of Scripture we discussed earlier, in which God asks Job where he was "when the morning stars sang together and all the sons of God shouted for joy" at the creation of all things (Job 38:7). The doctrine of creation reminds us that there really is something *musical* about the cosmos. For if people are silent, even the rocks will cry out, singing the glory of their maker and joining the song of all creation as God's handiwork *declares* the glory of God (Ps. 19:1–7; Luke 19:40). Or, as Psalm 96 puts it, "Let the heavens be glad, and let the earth rejoice; let the sea roar, and all that fills it; let the field exult, and everything in it! *Then shall all the trees of the forest sing for joy*" (vv. 11–12).

My worry for all of us is that our lives are too busy and our ears are filled with too much noise for our souls to be tuned to the frequency of the cosmos's song. However, there are moments, like Jamieson and Rosa describe using the idea of *resonance*, when our souls catch the song. When this happens, something inside us bursts with meaning, and we know, even

7. Bobby Jamieson, *Everything Is Never Enough: Ecclesiastes' Surprising Path to Resilient Happiness* (Waterbrook, 2025), 176.

if only for a second, that we are acting in line with our status and place as creatures in God's good creation.

We are all hardwired to long for truth, beauty, and goodness. It is a product of our being created by the supremely good One—who, after creating, looked out over his creation and called it good (Gen. 1:31)—and why we follow the One who is in himself the way, the truth, and the life (John 14:6). The deepest desire of our souls is captured in the words of David: "*One thing* have I asked . . . that I may dwell in the house of the LORD . . . to gaze upon [your] beauty" (Ps. 27:4). We desire truth, beauty, and goodness because we worship the One who is the ground of and is himself truth, beauty, and goodness. He has created us to resonate with the way the world *ought* to hum.

At the same time, the doctrine of creation reminds us—for all the stable and wise resonance we may feel in this world—that we were nonetheless created for another world. Jamieson, discussing how this is not a flaw with the way God has ordered the cosmos but a key feature of it, writes:

> The problem with stuffing the vastness of eternity into the cramped compartments of the human heart is that it doesn't fit. What God has put inside us guarantees an enduring mismatch between what we want and what this world can give. . . . The human heart is pierced with a hole that lets in the infinite. That is why all the finite goods that our toil gains fail to satisfy.[8]

Or, to keep our theme of C. S. Lewis going in this chapter, a theme that will also continue in the next point: "If I find in myself a desire which no experience in this world can satisfy, the most probable explanation is that I was made for another world."[9]

8. Jamieson, *Everything Is Never Enough*, 83.
9. Lewis, *Mere Christianity*, 136–37.

Having wisdom regarding the doctrine of creation permits stability in the Christian life. We can know that creation has a purpose, and we can *resonate* with that very purpose as we tune our souls to the frequency of the cosmos. Moreover, there are stability and wisdom found in knowing that as beautiful as the song creation sings, it is a mere foreshadowing of the true song of the saints we will sing to God's glory when we cross the Jordan.

Creation and Faithfulness

I opened this chapter with a quote from *The Magician's Nephew* in which Aslan sings Narnia into existence. There is another quote from that same scene that shows both a correct response to the doctrine of creation and just how well Lewis captures theological realities in his fiction. One of the handful of characters in the scene is the Cabby, a character with a surprising story arc who is introduced as a simple London cab driver. As he witnesses Aslan singing creation into being, the Cabby exclaims, "Glory Be! . . . I'd ha' been a better man all my life if I'd known there were things like this."[10]

There is something profound here. When we survey all Scripture has to say about the doctrine of creation, it makes the Cabby's response all the more beautiful. This simple man realized that the splendor of creation ought to have caused him to be a better man than he was throughout his life; he'd just never had the eyes to see it. In Scripture, when any notion of God's creating the world is brought up, it is done so to invoke fidelity and faithfulness in God's people. In fact, I am convinced this is a far too neglected aspect of the Christian understanding of creation. We serve the One who breathed out the stars and who tells the ocean where to stop. If we could have witnessed the miraculous acts described in God's response to Job, we, too,

10. Lewis, *Magician's Nephew*, 107.

like the Cabby, would recognize that we could spend our days being far better men and women.

Consider just a few passages that show how the doctrine of creation ought to rouse faithfulness in God's people. These passages are examples that the doctrine of creation ought to remind us that God is in control and that his providence extends over all the cosmos. Since he is the One who, out of the plenitude of his own life, created the cosmos, we can trust him with our day-to-day lives, and as our souls are reminded of his creative power, we remember to bend our knees to his will.

When Moses wants the people of Israel to remember God's faithfulness, he reminds them, "When you are in tribulation, and all these things come upon you in the latter days, you will return to the LORD your God and *obey his voice*. For the LORD your God is a merciful God. He will not leave you or destroy you or forget the covenant with your fathers that he swore to them" (Deut. 4:30–31). To press this truth deeper into their hearts, Moses then points them back to creation itself, saying, "For ask now of the days that are past, which were before you, since the day that God created man on the earth, and ask from one end of heaven to the other, whether such a great thing as this has ever happened or was ever heard of" (4:32).

The prophet Amos also uses creation to show just how wicked the sins of Israel were as God brought hardship against them in their refusal to return to covenant faithfulness: "For behold, he who forms the mountains and creates the wind, and declares to man what is his thought, who makes the morning darkness, and treads on the heights of the earth—the LORD, the God of hosts, is his name!" (Amos 4:13).

Another prophet, Malachi, recalls the notion of creation for the sake of calling God's people to ethical faithfulness: "Have we not all one Father? Has not one God created us? Why then are we faithless to one another, profaning the covenant of our fathers? Judah has been faithless, and abomination has been committed in Israel and in Jerusalem" (Mal. 2:10–11). Yet, it is not just for judgment that the prophets remind God's people of creation. Isaiah, for instance, uses creation to move people in the opposite direction—to rouse confidence and assurance in his hearers:

> But now thus says the LORD,
> he who created you, O Jacob,
> he who formed you, O Israel:
> "Fear not, for I have redeemed you;
> I have called you by name, you are mine.
> When you pass through the waters, I will be with you.
> . . .
> Fear not, for I am with you;
> I will bring your offspring from the east,
> and from the west I will gather you.
> I will say to the north, Give up,
> and to the south, Do not withhold;
> bring my sons from afar
> and my daughters from the end of the earth." (Isa. 43:1–2, 5–6)

The theme of thinking about God's creative act to stir faithfulness continues into the New Testament as well. Whether it is the author of Hebrews declaring that Christ is the fullness of revelation and the One through whom God created the world and who "upholds the universe by the word of his power" (Heb. 1:3) or Paul saying "all things were created through him and for him" (Col. 1:16), both authors use Christ's active participation in creation to spur readers to wonder and worship.

To close this chapter, we would be wise to learn from the psalms and have the pattern in our own lives of remembering the work of God's hands. As King David writes, "I remember the days of old; I meditate on all that you have done; I ponder the work of your hands" (Ps. 143:5). Like David, we should pause to contemplate the splendor of creation and let its beauty serve as a tutor, lifting our minds to the Creator. Early church father Basil of Caesarea knew the correct path of using the things of this world to discipline our minds about the Creator of this world, writing, "[Creation] is really the school where reasonable souls exercise themselves, the training ground where they learn to know God; since by the sight of visible and sensible things the mind is led, as by a hand, to the contemplation of invisible things."[11]

So, then, with our minds having considered creation but also being trained *by* creation, we lift our mind's eye toward the Creator of all and join in the song of the cosmos:

> Praise him, sun and moon,
> praise him, all you shining stars!
> Praise him, you highest heavens,
> and you waters above the heavens!
> Let them praise the name of the Lord!
> For he commanded and they were created. (Ps. 148:3–5)

11. Basil of Caesarea, "Hexameron," in *Nicene and Post-Nicene Fathers Second Series*, vol. 1, ed. Philip Schaff and Henry Wace (Hendrickson, 2007), 6.

4

Scripture

Delighting in Your Authority

If our deepest joy is found in knowing God, then we are blessed beyond measure that God has made himself known. God has given us sixty-six books revealing who he is and what he is doing in our world. Christians confess that Scripture is inspired—breathed out by God himself. The very words of Scripture are not merely the product of human thought but of the Spirit, who carried along the prophets and the apostles to write precisely what God intended (2 Pet. 1:21). Put simply, to consider the Christian doctrine of Scripture is to recognize that when Scripture speaks, God himself speaks.

Even the very nature of Scripture as a written text is miraculous. Spanning some fifteen hundred years of authorship, written by over thirty authors, constructed in three languages, containing nearly every genre of literature imaginable, the Bible in its uniqueness is nearly impossible to match. What is more, in all this diversity, these various voices, languages, and genres do not collide to form a cacophony of disunity but together are a symphony of harmony proclaiming the goodness and glory of a God who has redeemed a wayward people in himself, through himself, and to himself.

Introducing the Doctrine of Scripture

In the words of Scripture, we hear not only the voice of God but also reality. We are met with a narrative bursting with truth, beauty, and goodness. These sixty-six God-breathed books are a narrative of the greatest story conceivable: God with us and God for us. But this story is not just a grand narrative but a personal one as well, for in these pages we find *our very own story*—how we are numbered among the sons of Adam and daughters of Eve who dared trespass a holy God. We read of his creation and how we've polluted it. We read of his law and how we've transgressed it. We read of his glory and how we've not comprehended it. We read of his redemption and how we've not deserved it. We read of his people and how we've been numbered among them. We read of the consummation of all things and how we have a day coming that is glorious beyond imagination.

We live in a noisy world with a thousand voices competing for our attention. The world can feel loud and enticing, but its voices do not know us and do not speak the truth. It is in the voice of God, as written in the Scriptures, where we will find the mirror to see our true selves and to see the world we inhabit as it truly is.[1]

God could have revealed himself in whatever way he desired. He could have made the birds of the air chirp the gospel in every language on earth; he could have made the clouds spell out the

1. This is a phrase from Kevin Vanhoozer and Daniel Treier, *Theology and the Mirror of Scripture: A Mere Evangelical Account* (IVP Academic, 2015).

truths contained in Scripture in the sky; he could have made his self-revelation fully contained in mere human intuition. But this is not the path he chose. Rather, he has revealed himself in a book. By consequence, we ought to be a *bookish* people. We ought to be especially interested in *this book*.

My hope here is simply to act as a tour guide for a brief journey considering the Holy Scriptures. The aim of this chapter is to help us begin thinking about both the uniqueness and the beauty of this book. In considering the wonder that is God's Word written down, may we all be convinced and confess, along with our Lord Jesus Christ, that "man shall not live by bread alone, but by every word that comes from the mouth of God" (Matt. 4:4).

Defining the Doctrine of Scripture

First, if we want to read any kind of literature correctly, one of the most important things we can do is know *what kind* of literature it is. This is a basic point but one that bears significance for approaching the Bible.

Bibliology Versus Hermeneutics

Consider a simple example to see the idea behind this point: Imagine I handed you a famous comic strip and then also handed you the eulogy of a relative of mine. You would know, rather instinctively, that you ought to read those two forms of literature with vastly different postures. The moment you saw the panels of the comic strip and realized what you were holding, you would know humor was involved. You would know to expect sarcasm and tongue-in-cheek writing with puns, jokes, quips, and sharp points baked in. If you brought that same kind of reading posture to the eulogy, the result would be strange and awkward. If you read it—something somber detailing significant moments in a deceased person's life—the same way you read the comic strip, you would miss the meaning of the eulogy altogether.

We can choose nearly any two forms of literature and do this same exercise: We do not read a Christmas card the same way we read a traffic ticket, or read a social media caption the same way we read a novel, or read a weather forecast the same way we read a recipe book. I could keep going, but the point should be clear by now: *What* a piece of literature is impacts *how* we read it. A more academic way to say the same point is that the ontology of literature impacts the function of that literature, or bibliology should always precede hermeneutics.[2] *What* the Scripture is should impact *how* we read that Scripture. Bibliology is the study of Scripture, especially concerning the "what" questions of Scripture, while hermeneutics deals with questions like "How do we read this text?" and "How do we draw meaning out of the text?"

Therefore, one of the most important questions we can ask about Scripture is simply "What is it?"

Five Attributes of Scripture

To answer this question, many strategies or answers could prove helpful, yet I would like to put forward one that considers the following five attributes of Scripture: inspiration, inerrancy, authority, sufficiency, and perspicuity. Considering these five key attributes of Scripture will not give us *everything* we want to say about what Scripture is but will give us a framework for making sense of the question. Moreover, these five attributes of Scripture not only will provide some handrails for questions of bibliology (the study of Scripture) but also will be sufficient springboards for considering how we can delight in the doctrine of Scripture. What I hope becomes clear is that Scripture

2. John Webster, *Holy Scripture: A Dogmatic Sketch* (Cambridge University Press, 2003), 6.

is God's self-disclosure in which he invites us into fellowship with himself as we read and partake in the narrative of the resurrected Christ, who is the apex of the unfolding drama. In God's economy of bringing wayward sinners to himself, his Word is a reliable communication inspired through the Holy Spirit. In his speech, we find inspired, inerrant, authoritative, sufficient, and clear testimony about the Triune God and all things in relation to the Triune God.

Attribute 1: Inspiration

The very basic building block we must first affirm about Scripture is that it is *God's Word*. Just as the type of literature impacts the way we handle that literature, so, too, does *who* the literature is from. For example, imagine I hand you a note from my five-year-old daughter. As I give it to you, you might think, *I'm sure this will be adorable*. Now, imagine I hand you a letter and say it is from God himself. Your thoughts, as you take the letter in your hand, would likely have more gravitas; you may think, *This is from the person I'd most want to hear from*.

Saying that Holy Scripture is speech directly from God revolutionizes the way we approach and define the text. Hear how two theologians, Scott Swain and Kevin Vanhoozer, detail this point. Swain writes, "In dealing with the Bible interpretively, we are not rational subjects dealing with an inert object; we are instead rational subjects addressed by the divine Subject and called to loving attention and fellowship."[3]

Swain is right to point out that we are not merely rational subjects dealing with an inert object. Think about how a scientist approaches research—there needs to be a built-in distance so that the scientist can make unbiased, objective decisions about raw material. While Bible reading may feel like

3. Scott Swain, *Trinity, Revelation, and Reading: A Theological Introduction to the Bible and Its Interpretation* (T&T Clark, 2011), 7.

this at times, in the end it should not be so. We approach the Bible not as mere material to be examined but as speech that calls us into communion. The proper analogy for the location of reading Scripture is not a laboratory for verbal dissection but a burning bush anticipating a divine encounter. And our response to Scripture should be not a distant examination of data but expectant exaltation in which Samuel's words ought to be ours: "Speak, Lord, for your servant hears" (1 Sam. 3:9).

Kevin Vanhoozer makes the point with clarity:

> Scripture requires more than parsing verbs, more than intellectual assent to its propositions, more even than application of its moral principles. There is nothing personal, or demanding, about data processing. Every divine speech act—indicative, interrogative, and imperative alike—poses a tacit question to the reader, namely, "How will you respond to what has been said and to the person who has said it?" . . . If we keep in mind what the Bible is for, our most important answer must be deeply personal, even existential: "Let it be to me according to your word" (Luke 1:38).[4]

Concursive Inspiration

There are two more theological ideas vital for a robust understanding of how God inspires Holy Scripture: concursive inspiration and verbal plenary inspiration. Let us consider the first one: To say that the inspiration of Scripture is a concursive inspiration is to say that the author of Scripture is God and the author of Scripture is human beings is not contradictory. Concursive inspiration means that all Scripture has a dual authorship—both God and humans wrote the sixty-six books of Scripture. In other words, God inspired every word of Scripture and superintended the construction of Scripture as he saw fit in his sovereign will; at the same time, the human authors

4. Kevin Vanhoozer, *Mere Christian Hermeneutics: Transfiguring What It Means to Read the Bible Theologically* (Zondervan Academic, 2024), 15.

of Scripture wrote the words of their various books with their freedom, creative integrity, and authorship fully intact. This means that the human authors of Scripture are truly "authors, not conduits: conscious, intelligent, [and] deliberate."[5] They made real decisions and wrote authentically, and yet God was guiding every word of their writing to carry forth his divine message. This means that the correct answer to a question like "Who wrote Romans, God or Paul?" would simply be yes.

There is much beauty in concursive dual authorship. This understanding of inspiration helps us make sense of a profound phenomenon in Scripture: its unity and diversity. On the one hand, we can say Scripture has one author—God—and since there is one consistent author throughout the book, there is one unified message heading in the same direction and toward the same end. And yet, since God spoke through thirty-plus authors spanning centuries and literary forms, there is vast diversity to the book that gives it a truly human feel. Few writers have thought about the beauty of this unity-through-diversity like theologian B. B. Warfield. About diversity, Warfield says:

> On first throwing open this wonderful volume we are struck immediately with the fact that it is not a book, but rather a congeries of books. No less than sixty-six separate compositions immediately stare us in the face. These treatises come from the hands of at least thirty distinct writers, scattered over a period of some fifteen hundred years, and embrace specimens of nearly every kind of writing known among men. Histories, codes of law, ethical maxims, philosophical treatises, discourses, dramas, songs, hymns, epics, biographies, letters both official and

5. John Webster, "ὑπὸ πνεύματος ἁγίου φερόμενοι ἐλάλησαν ἀπὸ θεοῦ ἄνθρωποι: On the Inspiration of Holy Scripture," in *Conception, Reception, and the Spirit: Essays in Honor of Andrew T. Lincoln*, ed. J. Gordon McConville and Lloyd K. Pietersen (Wipf & Stock, 2015), 246.

> personal, vaticinations—every kind of composition known beneath heaven seems gathered here in one volume.[6]

Notice the categories of diversity Warfield mentions. The Scriptures have thirty-plus authors spread out over fifteen hundred years. To put this span of time in perspective, this would be like early church father Augustine starting a book and modern fantasy author J. K. Rowling finishing the book. Beyond the time span, there are vastly different *kinds* of literature in Scripture, from legal codes to poetry.

And yet, with all the grand diversity throughout the book, there is one Author inspiring the many authors and one Story woven through the many stories. Listen to Warfield now describe not the diversity but the *unity* of Scripture:

> We may look, however, on a still greater wonder. Let us once penetrate beneath all this primal diversity and observe the internal character of the volume, and a most striking unity is found to pervade the whole; so that, in spite of having been thus made up of such diverse parts, it forms but one organic whole. . . . The same doctrine is taught from beginning to end, running like a golden thread through the whole and stringing book after book upon itself like so many pearls.[7]

Before we leave Warfield, there is one more crucial insight the Princeton theologian gives us regarding Scripture and God's inspiration of it. In one of his magisterial essays, "It Says:" "Scripture Says:" "God Says:," Warfield masterfully shows how Scripture is totally comfortable using these three phrases rather interchangeably.[8] This shows that Scripture is willing to call the

6. B. B. Warfield, "The Divine Origin of the Bible," in *Revelation and Inspiration* (P&R, 1882), 436.

7. Warfield, "Divine Origin of the Bible," 436.

8. B. B. Warfield, "'It Says:' 'Scripture Says:' 'God Says:'," in *Revelation and Inspiration*, 283–334.

words of a human author "God's words," and vice versa. To see the profundity of this point, consider an example:

> Therefore, as the Holy Spirit says,
>
> > "Today, if you hear his voice,
> > do not harden your hearts as in the rebellion,
> > on the day of testing in the wilderness,
> > where your fathers put me to the test
> > and saw my works for forty years." (Heb. 3:7–9)

Notice who the author of Hebrews attributes these words to: "the Holy Spirit." But what is fascinating is that the author goes on to quote Psalm 95:7–11. It is easy to miss how profound this is: The author of Hebrews seems totally comfortable saying the words of David *are the words of the Holy Spirit*. This could be the case only if God the Spirit inspired David to write the psalm. So then, did God or David write Psalm 95? Yes.

An example also goes the other way. In Romans 9:17, Paul writes, "For the *Scripture says* to Pharaoh, 'For this very purpose I have raised you up.'" However, readers familiar with the Old Testament will know these are the words the Lord instructed Moses to say to Pharaoh, and if we revisit the original citation, God is the one talking here (Exod. 9:16). This means Paul is comfortable calling God's words "Scripture." As Warfield shows, "it says," "Scripture says," and "God says" seem to have some interchangeability in the text, which is remarkable evidence that what we have in Scripture is God's Word.

Yet, all this is but a theological reflection of what Scripture says outright. Paul writes in his second letter to Timothy, "All Scripture is *breathed out by God* and profitable for teaching, for reproof, for correction, and for training in righteousness" (2 Tim. 3:16). Likewise, Peter writes, "Knowing this first of all, that no prophecy of Scripture comes from someone's own interpretation. For no prophecy was ever produced by the will of man, but men spoke from God *as they were carried along by the Holy Spirit*" (2 Pet. 1:20–21).

Verbal Plenary Inspiration

Now that we have established that God's Word was written by both God and man, it will prove important to turn to our second theological term for the doctrine of inspiration: verbal plenary inspiration. When considering how God inspired the text of Scripture through human authors, we find several views as to *what* exactly is inspired.[9] The view I find most faithful to the biblical text and that gives Christians a robust confidence that what they read in their Bibles is the Word of the Lord is a view called verbal plenary inspiration.

This view is best understood by simply breaking down the two words *verbal* and *plenary*. *Verbal* means that God's superintendence, or oversight, of Scripture extends down to the very words chosen—not merely the ideas of Scripture. Some views suggest that God inspired *ideas* in the minds of the human authors, but as the authors wrote the books, the words were not of divine inspiration. This allows for errors in the text, as there could be a less-than-ideal word choice so long as the *ideas* are communicated well. The verbal plenary view of inspiration denies that only the *ideas* of Scripture are inspired by God; the ideas and the very *words* are intentional. Saying the very words of Scripture are intentional means that believers can know there is not one wasted word in their Bibles and that *all Scripture* is breathed out by God and useful (2 Tim. 3:16).

The second word, *plenary*, simply means "all." To say that God's inspiration extends to all Scripture means that every book, every chapter, every section, every verse, and every word is inspired by God. From Genesis to Revelation, it is all God-breathed. There are faulty views of inspiration that suggest that

9. For a brief explanation of varying views, see David Dockery and Malcolm Yarnell III, *Special Revelation and Scripture* (B&H Academic, 2024), 153–58.

only the portions of the Bible that relay information needed for salvation or particular doctrines are inspired. The verbal plenary view of inspiration denies this idea. On the contrary, this view asserts that, down to the very word, *all* Scripture is inspired by God. When we open our Bibles, we are not just reading *about* God; we are preparing our hearts and minds to hear *from* God.

Attribute 2: Inerrancy

Following the conviction that knowing *what kind* of literature and *who* the literature is from impacts what we think about *how* the literature functions, we come to the doctrine of inerrancy. To put it in its simplest terms, inerrancy teaches that Scripture is truth without any mixture of error. Since God is the speaker and God is truth, and since speech reflects the character of the speaker, God's speech is truth (Num. 23:19; Ps. 119:160; John 14:6; 17:17).

While a definition of "true without any mixture of error" is sufficient for a basic understanding of what it means for Scripture to be inerrant, I have come to appreciate John Feinberg's careful definition of the doctrine:

> Inerrancy means that when all facts are known, the Scriptures in their original autographs and properly interpreted will be shown to be wholly true in everything that they affirm, whether that has to do with doctrine or morality or with the social, physical, or life sciences.[10]

While many nuances of this definition are worth pursual, I'd like to simply point out a few. Notice the caveats: (1) all the facts are known, (2) the original autographs, and (3) proper interpretation. Some may claim that narrowing the doctrine

10. John Feinberg, *Light in a Dark Place: The Doctrine of Scripture* (Crossway, 2018), 237.

of inerrancy by this trifold nuance minimizes the claim that Scripture is free from error, but I disagree. In fact, these needed nuances demonstrate that not every *reading* of the biblical text is without error; rather, the text itself is error-free. Connected with divine inspiration, biblical inerrancy means that the Scriptures, in their original manuscripts and as they have been faithfully transmitted from one generation to the next, are wholly trustworthy and free from error in all they affirm.

This commitment to divine inerrancy, as stated in the definition above, extends to *all* Scripture. This means that whatever Scripture intends to address, it does so in an authoritative, trustworthy, and error-free manner. This should be understood to extend to domains including doctrine, morality, social sciences, physical sciences, and life sciences. Inerrancy is not confined to one domain. Whatever area of life Scripture speaks to, it speaks without error. This also means that we should *not* render the ethics of Scripture as merely cultural, as if the moralistic claims of the sacred Scriptures may have been true for a time but not for our time. Rather, *whatever* Scripture says, it says without mixture of error. Its doctrinal, salvific, ethical, and empirical claims are made in a way that matches the nature of its speaker—one of truth.[11]

There are many other nuances and claims worthy of consideration when it comes to the vital doctrine of biblical inerrancy, but I want to bring this brief discussion to a close by showing that affirming the Scriptures' truthfulness is not a new phenomenon in the history of the church. While the nineteenth and twentieth centuries demanded sustained attention and careful exposition of exactly what the church means when we say that the biblical material is infallible and inerrant, proclaiming the truthfulness and the dangers of denying such truthfulness is not

11. For an exposition on what it means for the Scriptures to be inerrant, readers should carefully work through and consider the nineteen affirmations and denials outlined in the Chicago Statement on Biblical Inerrancy.

so new. As one example among many, hear Augustine writing around AD 394 on the subject:

> I think it is extremely dangerous to admit that anything in the Sacred Books should be a lie; that is, that the men who have composed and written the Scriptures for us should have lied in their books. . . . If we once admit in that supreme authority even one well-intentioned lie, there will be nothing left of those books, because, whenever anyone finds something difficult to practice or hard to believe, he will follow this most dangerous precedent and explain it as the idea or practice of a lying author.[12]

Attribute 3: Authority

The authority of Scripture grounds the believer's life and doctrine in something greater than mere human intuition, ecclesial authority, or cultural trends. While there are lesser authorities that ought to operate in our lives, we hold that Scripture alone is the *final* authority in all things pertaining to life and godliness. Given our belief in the inspiration of Scripture, we believe that when Scripture speaks, God speaks, and therefore, as we hear the Word of God in Scripture, we must bend the knee to its authority over us. Scott Swain serves readers well as he articulates just how authoritative the Bible is for norming the Christian life:

> Scripture stands as the supreme authority for faith and life. The Bible is not simply the vehicle through which God issues his authoritative Word in the church. It is the supreme enunciation of God's authoritative Word in the church, short of the Lord's return. In Holy Scripture God provides the authentic self-presentation of his name, issues his authoritative declaration of the gospel, and publishes his will for Christian life, ministry, and

12. Augustine, *Augustine's Commentary on Galatians: Introduction, Text, Translation, and Notes*, ed. Eric Plumer (Oxford University Press, 2003), 48.

> worship. Because God not only speaks through Scripture but in Scripture, Scripture bears intrinsic authority and warrants our absolute submission. Scripture's claims are God's claims, and thus command our assent (Rev. 19:9). Scripture's promises are God's promises, and thus command our trust (Titus 1:2–3). Scripture's instructions are God's instructions, and thus command our obedience (Matt. 15:3–4). The one who trembles at God's Word honors God and receives his favor (Isa. 66:2). Conversely, the one who despises God's Word despises God and incites his wrath (Matt. 15:1; cf. Isa. 29:13).[13]

It is common, when we begin to think about Scripture's authority in-depth for the first time, to wonder how Scripture's authority relates to other authorities in our lives or if we should even *have* other authorities in our lives. Protestants affirm the vital doctrine flowing from the Protestant Reformation of *sola scriptura*—Scripture alone. So, how might we think of other authorities if Scripture *alone* is our authority? This question has led some well-meaning Christians to argue that we should not have doctrinal statements, creeds, or confessions in our churches or personal lives since Scripture is our authority. The worry is that upholding creeds or confessions would multiply authority in our lives and ascribe authority to a creed that only the Bible should have. This is where we hear the mantra "No creed but the Bible" or "No creed but Christ."

I want to applaud Christians who feel this way for their unwaveringly high view of Scripture. Yet, I think this is a position that mistakes the doctrine of *sola scriptura*—Scripture alone—for a lesser doctrine of *solo scriptura*, or *only* Scripture. This distinction may seem like semantics or a mere playing with words, yet it is an important one. While *sola scriptura* says that Scripture *alone* can be our final authority on all things pertaining to life and godliness, *solo scriptura*, on the contrary, says

13. Swain, *Trinity, Revelation, and Reading*, 73.

that Scripture can be our *only* authority for things pertaining to life and godliness. While it may be easy to miss, *sola scriptura* has room for *lesser* authorities to aid Christians as they follow Christ in faithfulness.

When discussing this issue with my students, I like to remind them how untenable a position that posits Scripture as their *only* authority is. For example, if my students left class and drove eighty miles per hour on the road outside the seminary, they would quickly be pulled over by a police officer. If they questioned that this police officer had any authority to act and hold them accountable based on their belief that *only* Scripture is authoritative, it would go poorly for them. While this is a silly example, we can extrapolate on the idea: For example, Scripture calls us to submit to the leaders of the church (Heb. 13:17), which seems to suggest that our local church pastors hold some kind of authority over us. What begins to become clear, rather fast, is that while "No creed but the Bible" sounds pious, it is itself a creed, just a poor one that will not protect God's people from error.

A robust doctrine of *sola scriptura* shows that Scripture is our *final* authority, and that while we do indeed have lesser authorities in our lives, they all must bend the knee to God's Word. Allow me to introduce a distinction that has been helpful for many throughout church history, including myself. The church, thinking about this very issue—how different authorities in our lives relate to one another—developed two Latin terms that bring about much clarity. The first is *norma normans*, and the second is *norma normata*. In English, *norma normans* translates roughly to "the norm that norms" or "the rule that rules." This means that this rule (or authority) rules all other authorities. So, those who believe in *sola scriptura* should place the Bible in this category. Sometimes you will see a longer version, *norma normans non normata*, which translates to "the norm that norms and is itself not normed." The Bible is a rule in our lives and an authority in our lives, and this particular authority has authority over all other authorities, and no other can have authority over it.

As for the second term—*norma normata*—this phrase, in English, translates roughly to "the norm that is normed" or "the rule that is ruled." Something in this category *does* have authority in our lives, but there is a higher authority that rules this authority. For example, our pastors should indeed have a healthy, biblically faithful authority over us as we submit to their pastoral care. However, while our pastors have authority over us, they have an authority over them—namely Jesus Christ, the true shepherd. Or while local police officers do indeed have some measure of authority over us as citizens, they have an authority over them that does not allow them to do whatever they please. The have a certain level of "rulership," but their rulership is "ruled" by someone else.

It is in this second category that we should place things like confessional statements and creeds. For example, at my local church, we affirm a confessional statement that our members must agree to in order to join our church. The statement brings unity, as we know where we all stand on a number of theological topics. Our church's confession has authority over us as a body of believers; if anyone begins to believe something outside our confession, the church has the authority to step in and hold those believers accountable. However, while the statement has authority over us, its authority is a derivative one. This means that we believe the confession is authoritative only because we find it to be a good summary of the Bible—our ultimate authority—and the Bible will always have the final say, not our confessional statement. So, the Bible is *norma normans* and the statement is *norma normata*.

I often use the following chart to show my students how various levels of authority work and how we can have a robust doctrine of the Bible's authority and still hold to lesser authorities.

Sola Scriptura and Levels of Authority

First Order Authority	*Norma Normans Non Normata* The norm that norms all norms and is itself not normed	God Scripture alone (*sola scriptura*)
Second Order Authority	*Norma Normata* The norm that is normed	Creeds Councils The church Doctrinal statements Elders, governing officials, etc.
Third Order Authority	—	Experience Opinion Intuition

Attribute 4: Sufficiency

About the sufficiency of Scripture, the Westminster Confession states:

> The whole counsel of God concerning all things necessary for his own glory, man's salvation, faith and life, is either expressly set down in Scripture, or by good and necessary consequence may be deduced from Scripture: unto which nothing at any time is to be added, whether by new revelations of the Spirit, or traditions of men (2 Tim. 3:15–17; Gal. 1:8–9; 2 Thess. 2:2). Nevertheless, we acknowledge the inward illumination of the Spirit of God to be necessary for the saving understanding of such things as are revealed in the Word (John 6:45; 1 Cor. 2:9–12) and that there are some circumstances concerning the worship of God, and government of the Church, common to human actions and societies, which are to be ordered by the light of nature, and Christian prudence, according to the general rules of the Word, which are always to be observed (1 Cor 11:13–14; 14:26, 40).[14]

14. James T. Dennison Jr., ed., "Westminster Confession of Faith," in *Reformed Confessions of the 16th and 17th Centuries in English Translation*, vol. 4, *1600–1693* (Reformation Heritage Books, 2014), 235.

You would be hard-pressed to find a better statement concerning the sufficiency of Scripture than this paragraph. It sets out a robust positive vision of why we believe Scripture is sufficient for the Christian life while providing the needed nuances of what it means to affirm a doctrine like sufficiency.

In explaining the doctrine of Scripture's sufficiency, I have found it helpful to clarify two things sufficiency does *not* mean and then turn toward articulating what it *does* mean. Two things the doctrine of sufficiency does *not* mean: (1) that Scripture tells us *everything* we need to know or do, and (2) that affirming the sufficiency of Scripture negates other sources of truth. These two denials may appear rather obvious, but given the misteachings and misunderstandings concerning this doctrine that abound today, they are worth saying. Moreover, these two negations can help shed light on the beauty of what sufficiency *does* mean.

First, to state that Scripture is sufficient is *not* to say that Scripture contains everything we need to know. We can read and reread the canon of Scripture, and it will never instruct us on which exact person to marry or which house to buy. The Scriptures do not prescribe a particular diet over others or tell us which bedtime ritual will get our kids to sleep through the night. The Scriptures simply never intended to instruct us on these matters. (That being said, the Scriptures *do* provide the truths needed to develop wisdom in order to make decisions like these.) Trying to force Scripture to address issues it never intended to address will often lead to legalism and a never-ending proliferation of extrabiblical mandates, requirements, and laws.

Second, the sufficiency of Scripture does *not* negate other sources of truth. While there may be some who argue that an affirmation of sufficiency ought to lead Christians to negate truths learned from science, social studies, anthropology, and the like, the doctrine does not necessitate we do so. The doctrine *does* mean that if any of these fields outright contradict the wisdom we derive from God's inspired Word, then we will go with the Word every time. Of course, these fields and others can lead us astray, and we should not deceive ourselves into thinking they are not following their own narratives and liturgies in some way. We can, however, seek to put these fields and all like them under the authority of the Scriptures and know that truth, beauty, and goodness lie in a thousand corners so long as they accord with the Word of God.

So, then, if biblical sufficiency does not mean these two things, what *does* it mean? I think the answer to that question is stated well in the definition from the Westminster Confession: "All things necessary for [God's] own glory, man's salvation, faith and life" are "either expressly set down in Scripture, or by good and necessary consequence may be deduced from Scripture."

This means that those who seek to follow Christ are not looking for some new revelation. We are not lacking in our content to know God, to know God's will, to love God, and to follow God. In Scripture, we find the gospel that saves, the wisdom that guides, and the promises that sustain. We need not chase secret revelations, continued prophecies, cultural trends, or human philosophies to fill in gaps that Scripture supposedly left behind. The canon is closed, and God has spoken. The church need not supplement God's Word with an alternative; rather, the church sits under God's Word.

I do like to draw students' attention to an important phrase: "All things necessary for life and godliness are either expressly set down in Scripture *or by good and necessary consequence* may be deduced from it." For example, the doctrine of the Trinity is never expressly stated, and that word does not appear in Scripture. Nowhere does Scripture say, "God is one in essence and three in person, each person *homoousia* with the other two, subsisting in eternal relation, and this we shall call the Trinity." But while we do not have a chapter and verse of Scripture we can point to in order to show the word *Trinity*, we nevertheless know that it is a good and biblical doctrine, given all that Scripture has to say about the Father, the Son, and the Spirit. Therefore, we come to know the doctrine of the Trinity by good and necessary consequence. The same could be said for doctrines such as divine simplicity, divine impassability, and many others in which we need to consult the entirety of Scripture.

Attribute 5: Perspicuity

Of the five attributes of Scripture discussed in this chapter, perspicuity may be the one fewest of us have heard of or thought about. While it is not itself a very clear word, the doctrine of perspicuity considers the clarity of the Bible. To say the Bible has perspicuity is to say the Bible is clear in what it communicates. To be sure, this does not mean the Bible is always easy to understand; rather, its saving message is clear enough to be attainable by anyone who seeks after it rightly. To start the discussion on perspicuity, it will prove helpful to turn to the language of the older confessions. Hear, for example, how the Westminster Confession and the Second London Baptist Confession of 1689 define the doctrine of perspicuity:

> All things in Scripture are not alike plain in themselves, nor alike clear unto all. Yet, those things that are necessary to be known, believed, and observed for salvation are so clearly propounded, and opened in some place of Scripture or another, that not only the learned, but the unlearned, in a due use of the ordinary means, may attain unto a sufficient understanding of them.[15]

15. Dennison, "The London Baptist Confession," in *Reformed Confessions*, 531–71. The Second London Baptist Confession of 1689, 1.7, reads the same as the Westminster Confession, 1.7.

Notice how the confessions begin with a declaration that not all things are "plain." However, the claim of perspicuity is narrower; not *everything* in Scripture is plain, but that which is necessary for salvation is, "in some place of Scripture or another," so clear that not only the educated but also the uneducated, with right reading, may understand it.

Its importance may not jump out at readers right away, but the doctrine of perspicuity is dear to the heart of Protestants. It affirms that God's Word is for *God's people*—not an elitist class like priests and bishops alone. To say that even the uneducated and spiritually immature among us can understand the saving message of the gospel in the Scriptures is to put the Bible where it belongs: in the hands of the people. This clarity does not deny the depth and richness of Scripture or the need for careful study, but perspicuity does insist that the core message of redemption is not veiled for only ecclesiastical authority to discover and dispense. While pastors, scholars, and teachers are indeed aids to help God's people read the Word rightly, all of us have the most important ingredient needed for biblical interpretation: the indwelling of the Holy Spirit, who will lead us into all truth (John 14:26; 16:13).

Moreover, the doctrine of perspicuity seems to naturally arise out of the Bible's own confession. For example, after the most well-known portion of the *Shema*—"Hear, O Israel: The LORD our God, the LORD is one" (Deut. 6:4)—the text instructs, "And these words that I command you today shall be on your heart. *You shall teach them diligently to your children*" (vv. 6–7). This implies that the commands of the Lord can be understood even by children. A same line of argument could apply to Paul's instructions for Timothy to "continue in what you have learned and have firmly believed, knowing from whom you learned it and how *from childhood you have been acquainted with the sacred writings*, which are able to make you wise for salvation through faith in Christ Jesus" (2 Tim. 3:14–15). These passages and others like them are testimonies showing that Psalm 19:7 is not lying to us when it tells us that the "testimony of the Lord is sure" and that it can "[make] wise *the simple.*"

The Bible is God's Word for God's people, and *all* God's people—from the most educated to the least educated—should spend their days turning its pages seeking the voice of our Triune God, the face of Jesus Christ, and the salvation that comes from him.

Delighting in the Doctrine of Scripture

There is a peculiar weariness that comes from living in an age of constant noise. News cycles whirl in breathless urgency, our devices deliver noise in unbroken sequence, cultural winds shift without warning, and places that once felt like solid ground dissolve beneath our feet. Our days are loud with noise and quiet in wisdom. The heat is often turned up to the highest levels while the light is dim; the passion is high, but the wisdom is low.

A Stable Lamp in Troubled Times

We are a people in desperate need of stability. In the whirlwind of chaos and noise, Scripture is a stable lamp in our troubled times. The psalmist's image of God's Word is that of a lamp unto our feet—illuminating our path (Ps. 119:105). While this is poetry in the highest order, it is also a survival image. Even in the darkest nights, there is a light guiding our steps. The voices and noise of the present age may never go completely silent, but they are put in their place when we truly walk in the light of this lamp. The chaotic noise of an unsteady world will fade to a low murmur if we allow our souls to be tuned to the frequency of the Shepherd's voice.

History bears witness to the stability of Scripture. Empires have risen and crumbled, philosophies have flourished then faded, yet God's Word remains unshaken. Throughout the centuries and across the continents of church history, God's Word has steadied his people's feet. When the early church faced persecution, when the medieval church mourned plagues, when the Reformers stood before kings, when the moderns battled the Enlightenment—through all these ages and any to come—God's Word guided his people and kept their feet from slipping (Ps. 66:9; Hab. 3:19). The Word of the Lord was sufficient to keep those Christians stable amid hardship, and it is able to sustain *us*. Whether in tragedy, triumph, or the regular rhythms of the mundane day-to-day, God's Word is not a theoretical lamp for theoretical feet but a light upon *our* feet.

And here is another great comfort: The lamp of Scripture is not steady because of our grip upon it. The light upon our feet is sure because it is the Word of the Lord. The great author of Scripture is the great sustainer of his people; his Word is one of the great gifts he has given us to steady our souls. The stability of Scripture is rooted in the stability of its author. From the opening salvo of Genesis to the final amen of Revelation, his speech is coherent, consistent, and complete. He will keep us in the light, and we will proclaim with the prophet Isaiah, "The grass withers, the flower fades, but the word of our God will stand forever" (Isa. 40:8).

Encountering God in His Word

It is easy to miss, but a significant implication of the doctrine of divine inspiration is that when we read the words of Scripture, since they are inspired by God, we are reading the words of God. Moreover, these are not just the words of God to a vague idea of "people" in general; this book contains God's Word for *God's people*—if you are in Christ, that includes you. As Paul says when writing about inspiration, the fact that the Bible is God-breathed means that it is "profitable for teaching, for reproof, for correction, and for training in righteousness, *that the man of God* may be complete, equipped for every good work" (2 Tim. 3:16–17). In other words, it is for you and me. Yes, it is primarily about God. Yes, it is for *all* his people. Yet, if we read Scripture as a distant story concerning someone else, we will not read it correctly, and it will fail to be divine speech calling us to a particular covenantal life and personal conformity to Christ.

This is why I appreciate Kevin Vanhoozer's appropriation of Martin Buber's distinction between an "I-it" and an "I-thou" relationship between the reader and the biblical text. This concept is not overly brilliant, but it is quite helpful to properly frame the way we ought to think about Scripture. We have an I-it relationship with much in our lives. An I-it relationship exists when we have a relationship with something that is a mere object. The relationship can be defined as rather cold or distant, often characterized by mere utility. For example, when I make my morning pour-over coffee, I have an I-it relationship with my coffee mug. It serves me and has a usefulness in my life. However, the relationship is not mutual or personal in any meaningful sense. There is a danger in treating the Bible like this: When the Bible is a distant object of mere moral lessons or vaguely related stories, it does not really claim our lives in any demanding way. If our relationship with the Bible is merely an I-it relationship, we can pursue Bible study the way we'd pursue any other kind of study: as a critic using a stale scientific method for mere analyzation and to make the Bible a tool of utility. This reading culture, as Vanhoozer calls it, gives the Bible no claim over us in an authoritative or personal way.

On the contrary, an I-thou relationship between the reader and the biblical text is altogether different. In an I-thou relationship, there is something deeply personal, something intimate and near. Reading the biblical text as a "thou" is recognizing that there is a speaker behind the speech, and that speaker is none other than God. This means when we approach the biblical text, we are not permitted to read it as a distant artifact that exists for mere dissection of theological ideas or intellectual propositions. Rather, we are to submit ourselves to the text, since *God* is addressing us through it. The idea that God is speaking in a covenantal and communicative way through his text ought to alter our reading posture. Divine inspiration moves us from being "over" the text in a position of examining to being submissively "under" the text in a position of exaltation.

To bring this point home, Vanhoozer uses the words of Søren Kierkegaard to discuss how reading the Bible "objectively," or in a way categorized by an I-it relationship in an academic way, can impede the personal cultivation and transformation that ought to come with Bible reading:

> Kierkegaard worried that too many Christians interpret the Bible "objectively" to defend themselves against the transformative potential of the text: "To be alone with Holy Scripture! I dare not! If I open it—any passage—it traps me at once; it asks me. . . . Have you done what you read there? . . . But one can also defend oneself against God's Word. . . . Take Holy Scripture, lock your door—but then take ten dictionaries, twenty-five commentaries, then you can read it, just as calmly and coolly as you read newspaper advertising."[16]

Vanhoozer continues elaborating on Kierkegaard's point:

> Kierkegaard knew from experience how easily spiritual procrastination can hide under the guise of scholarly busyness. If even the scholars disagree about how to read the Bible, who am I to prefer my own opinion? A passage can have no claim on us if we are unable to determine what exactly it is saying.[17]

In conclusion, the God who spoke the cosmos into existence is the same God who now speaks, through the Bible, to his

16. Vanhoozer, *Mere Christian Hermeneutics*, 15–16.
17. Vanhoozer, *Mere Christian Hermeneutics*, 16.

people—including *you and me*. This is true not just for the so-called red-letter parts or the grand narratives alone—it's also true for the genealogies, the laws, the laments, and the letters. Every word bears the weight of divine authority and demands our obedience. Because God the Holy Spirit carried the prophets and apostles along so that every word written was superintended by God himself, the Bible is the book that we Christians should spend our days consuming. In this inspired book, we hear from God in a speech that is without admixture of error, authoritative over every other authority, sufficient for all things pertaining to life and godliness, and clear enough that sustained attention upon the words of this book will cultivate our souls and lead us in the way of salvation.

The Grace of Divine Accommodation

While it may seem an odd place to end the section on delighting in Scripture, I'd like to mention another doctrine pertaining to the Scriptures called divine accommodation. This doctrine, when considered with care, is a treasure trove of delight. Think back with me to our discussion of the doctrine of divine incomprehensibility: God is wholly other than us, and as he is infinite and we are finite, we can never comprehend the fullness of God. Yet, though God is incomprehensible, God has not left us without a way of meaningfully and truly knowing him. This is where the doctrine of incomprehensibility meets the doctrine of Scripture—through the highway of divine accommodation.

Remember our discussion of Exodus 33? This mysterious passage gives us a glimpse of the majesty of an incomprehensible God making himself knowable. Moses is talking with the Lord atop Mt. Sinai and requests to see his glory. God responds, "You cannot see my face, for man shall not see me and live" (v. 20). This response is *not* the same thing as God saying no. In fact, think of two other ways God could have responded. First, when Moses said, "Show me your glory," God could have said,

"Okay," and done so. This would have killed Moses, as seeing God in all his glory is fatal for his creatures. Luckily for Moses, this is not what God did. On the other hand, when Moses said, "Show me your glory," God could have said, "Absolutely not. You cannot handle seeing anything of my glory—it is simply too much for you."

God did not choose either of these options—to reveal all or to reveal nothing. Rather, he chose something in between: to reveal his glory to Moses in a way that accommodated Moses's creatureliness. God instructed the prophet,

> Behold, there is a place by me where you shall stand on the rock, and while my glory passes by I will put you in a cleft of the rock, and I will cover you with my hand until I have passed by. Then I will take away my hand, and you shall see my back, but my face shall not be seen. (vv. 21–23)

God wants to be known and reveals a glimpse of his glory to Moses, but he does so in a way that is mindful of Moses's creatureliness. As he did for Moses, he has done for you and me. Though he is incomprehensible, God uses language, images, and metaphors that are fitting for us. For example, God describes himself as having humanlike parts—even though he is spirit and has no body—so that you and I, as embodied creatures, might understand his revelation. Scripture discusses his eyes (Deut. 11:12), feet (Gen. 3:8), arms (Ps. 89:10), wings (Jer. 49:22), tongue (Isa. 30:27), and more. The list could go on for some time; God describes himself often with body parts he does not actually have. Why does he do this? It is for you; it is for me. It is for those of us who live our lives confined by bodies and can relate to what it means when God says, "I will strengthen you, I will help you, *I will uphold you with my righteous right hand*" (Isa. 41:10). We know what it would mean to be held on to by God's "righteous right hand." It helps us imagine the strength with which God has us in his grasp, which invokes our assurance in his hands. But do not miss that God does not actually have a right hand. In this description from Isaiah, God is *accommodating* us finite creatures who need a mental image like a strong hand. This is but one of the many ways God accommodates his otherness in Scripture in order to make himself not comprehensible but apprehensible to us creatures.

One of my favorite things to point out about God's accommodation of his creatures is that the Bible itself is *a story of grace*—a story of a God who had everything and needed nothing redeeming those who had nothing and needed everything. While the Bible is indeed that—a story of grace—it is easy to miss that the Bible itself is *grace in its existence*. The Bible tells us a story of a gracious God, but even the way the Bible was written shows this gracious God in action; he reveals his majestic glory in a way that is fitting and accommodating to us creatures.[18]

18. While it would be worthwhile to work through the many other places in the Bible God accommodates himself through anthropomorphisms, we simply do not have the space. It will have to suffice for me to quote Herman Bavinck, who has compiled an impressive list to show just how prevalent this reality is in Scripture:

> But anthropomorphism in Scripture is even much more extensive. All that pertains to humans and even to creatures in general is also attributed to God. . . . God is said to have a soul (Lev 26:11) and a Spirit (Gen 1:2; Mt 12:28; etc.). . . . There is mention of his face (Ex 33:20, 23; Is 63:9; Ps 16:11; Mt 18:10; Rev 22:4), his eyes (Ps 11:4; Heb 4:13), his eyelids (Ps 11:4), the apple of his eye (Deut 32:10; Ps 17:8; Zech 2:8), his ears (Ps 55:3), his nose (Deut 33:10), his mouth (Deut 8:3), his lips (Job 11:5), his tongue (Is 30:27), his neck (Jer 18:17), his arm (Ex 15:16), his hand (Num 11:23), his right hand (Ex 15:12), his finger (Ex 8:19), his heart (Gen 6:6), his intestines (Is 63:15; Jer 31:20; Luke 1:78), his bosom (Ps 74:11; Jn 1:18), his feet (Is 66:1). (Bavinck, *Reformed Dogmatics*, vol. 2, ed. John Bolt [Baker Academic, 2004], 100)

5

Incarnation

Delighting in Your Savior

Jesus Christ is the cornerstone of the Christian faith. In my undergraduate classes, when I get to the unit on Christology—or the study of Christ—I often begin by recognizing there is a danger when throwing the suffix *-ology* onto the name Christ. The danger in putting *-ology* on anything is that it can immediately move it into a stale field of study. Thinking about Christ as a field of study makes it tempting to put Christ under an academic microscope that we may examine and dissect him in order to arrive at intellectual conclusions. May it never be! Christ, the second person of the Trinity and our Lord and Savior, will not merely be examined but must be exalted; he will not merely be parsed but must be praised; he will not merely be intellectually worked over but must be worshiped.

Introducing the Doctrine of the Incarnation

To begin, let us work to right-size our view of the One we're talking about so that this chapter on the incarnation becomes not a sterile lab of observation but kindling that sets our worship ablaze. When we enter into the field that is Christology, we are talking about the King of the cosmos. He is the treasure of all history. He is the Creator and sustainer of all things. He upholds the universe by the word of his power—and even as you read this very sentence, you are being sustained by his say-so. He is the one mediator between God and humankind, and it is only by his name that we may be saved. He is the radiance of the glory of God and the image of the invisible God. He is the One who emptied himself to the point of death and the One whom the prophets long foretold, and when we behold his face, we see the very face of God. There are no superlatives that can adequately describe his worth; there is no exaggerating his excellencies. He is the King of Kings, the Lord of all. Without Jesus Christ we have nothing, and with him we have everything.

In any other field of study, it would be wildly inappropriate to worship that which we study. When it comes to Christology, however, it is not just appropriate to worship Christ but commanded. We proceed, then, not so much by considering a few doctrines about Christ in order to establish our intellectual sophistication but as those searching for on-ramps to worship.

In this chapter, while there is much more that could be considered in Christology, we are going to look primarily at Christ's incarnation, that cosmic-changing event in which the second person of the Trinity took on flesh and dwelled among us. To do so, I would like to cover a few doctrines that may be new to many readers and bear theological names that can feel intimidating, but if we move past the intimidation and press in to their meaning, there is much beauty to be seen.

The road map for this chapter will be to look at the following:

1. The *hypostatic union*—or how Christ's human and divine natures are united in one person.

2. The *extra Calvinisticum*—or how Christ's human and divine natures are both operational and performing glorious work appropriate for that nature.
3. *Dyothelitism*—or how Christ's human and divine natures each possess a will and how this is helpful for Bible reading and also illuminates the gospel of grace.

Again, my assumption is that these words will be new for many readers, so I aim to provide clear definitions that give way to seeing why the doctrine is beautiful.

Defining the Doctrine of the Incarnation

In 1857, the great Baptist preacher Charles Spurgeon, preaching on the wonder of the incarnation from 2 Corinthians 8:9, exclaimed, "The Infinite has become an infant."[1] That statement should astound us. Of course, we are familiar with the news: Jesus Christ of Nazareth, a carpenter with a lowly story, was born in a manger since there was no room for his mother, Mary, to have him elsewhere. However, as often as the story is told, we ought not let familiarity dull the scandal of the incarnation. The carpenter of the cosmos—who crafted the stars and lights of the highest heavens—condescended and became a carpenter from Nazareth. What can become a tale we half-heartedly celebrate during the Christmas season should shock our souls and confound our intellects.

In an attempt to win at least *some* of the scandal of the incarnation back, I present some of the divine attributes we discussed in chapter 2 and what they mean for the incarnation:

> In his divinity he is the God without parts; in his humanity he is made of parts—bone, and blood, and body.

1. Charles H. Spurgeon, "The Condescension of Christ," in *New Park Street Pulpit*, vol. 3 (Passmore & Alabaster, 1855), 349.

In his divinity he is God who never changes; in his humanity he is changing every second as he gets older and wiser.
In his divinity he is God without passions; in his humanity he grieves over the death of his friend Lazarus.
In his divinity he is everywhere present; in his humanity he is singularly, locally present.
In his divinity he knows everything; in his humanity he grows in wisdom and knows not the time or the hour.
In his divinity he has life in himself and has no lack or limitation; in his humanity he is dependent upon a nursing mother to sustain his life.
In his divinity he is the infinite God without measure; in his humanity he is measurable, with finite parameters like height and weight.

We could run this same exercise for all the divine attributes. This is, of course, another way to say that, in the incarnation, Jesus is truly God and truly man. Everything that it means for him to be truly divine, *he is*. Everything that it means for him to be truly human, *he is*. The hard part for our minds, when considering Christ in his incarnation, is holding these together simultaneously. The incarnation is the scandalous news of the second person of the Trinity, the eternal Son of God, taking on flesh and becoming the temporal son of Mary.

While we will likely never fully wrap our minds around how Christ is one person with two natures, both divine and human *at the same time*, understanding a few important points of theology regarding the incarnation will nevertheless help us apprehend this mystery.

The Hypostatic Union: Christ and His Two Natures

The hypostatic union is one of the most helpful doctrines when considering how to properly think and speak about

Christ's incarnation. The Greek word *hypostasis* is significant in church history. If you read the primary and secondary material surrounding the early church, you can see there seemed to be some flexibility as to what exactly the term meant. However, while that history is important, it is not our focus here. So, with *many* in church history, we should affirm that this word is best translated as "person." The early church spent much time and debate considering exactly how two "natures" are united in this one *hypostasis*—or person. How is it possible that the second *person* of the Trinity, who now assumes a second nature—a human nature—is *one* person with *two* natures? That is the question behind the hypostatic union. There are additional questions as well, such as: How do we think about the relationship between these two natures? Do both natures keep their own individual properties, or do they blend together somehow? Are both natures at work in the same moment, or does just one act at a time? These questions and many like them circulated in the early church. We, as those living over two thousand years after the death of Christ, ought to be thankful for those Christians who came before us who sought to be faithful to the biblical text regarding our confession of Christ. There is much we can learn from this cosmic conversation about Christ, if we will listen—even if we do not feel much affinity for church history.

One such event in which the church pursued faithfulness in how to keep the natures of Christ together in a biblical way was the Council of Chalcedon, the fourth major council of the church. The council took place in AD 451 and focused on the confession of Christ as *one* person with *two* natures. The council and its conclusion—called the Chalcedonian Definition—help protect our confession about who Christ is in his incarnation.

When teaching the history and conclusions of this great council, I have found it helpful to show how the council protects and promotes four biblical teachings about Christ. These four claims about Christ are what we, as those who want to have a biblical Christology, ought to affirm in our own theology as well. The four claims are these:

1. Jesus is truly God.
2. Jesus is truly human.
3. Jesus is one person.
4. Jesus has two natures.[2]

Each of these statements contradicts an early church heresy—or a misteaching about the person of Christ. While it would be beneficial to work through the variegated church history regarding these four claims, it will have to suffice to say that claim one is contrary to the *Arian* heresy, claim two is contrary to the *Apollinarian* heresy, claim three is contrary to the *Nestorian* heresy, and claim four is contrary to the *Eutychian* heresy. The last two will receive more attention below.

All who have tried know just how difficult it is to articulate a robustly biblical doctrine of Christ in a way that avoids these four misteachings; however, the conclusion of the Council of Chalcedon has done just that. In a single paragraph, the Chalcedonian Definition gives the church biblical and confessional guardrails that keep our confession about Christ faithful to what Scripture reveals about him. Here is that definition, in full:

> Following the saintly fathers, we all with one voice teach the confession of one and the same Son, our Lord Jesus Christ: the same perfect in divinity and perfect in humanity, the same

2. These four claims are from Fred Sanders's helpful illustration, "The Chalcedonian Box." See his chapter "Introduction to Christology: Chalcedonian Categories for the Gospel Narrative," in *Jesus in Trinitarian Perspective*, ed. Fred Sanders and Klaus Issler (B&H Academic, 2007), 24.

> truly God and truly man, of a rational soul and a body; consubstantial with the Father as regards his divinity, and the same consubstantial with us regards his humanity; like us in all respects except for sin; begotten before the ages from the Father as regards his divinity, and in the last days the same for us and for our salvation from Mary, the virgin God-bearer, as regards his humanity; one and the same Christ, Son, Lord, Only-begotten, acknowledged in two natures which undergo no confusion, no change, no division, no separation; at no point was the difference between the natures taken away through the union, but rather the property of both natures is preserved and comes together into a single person and a single subsistent being; he is not parted or divided into two persons, but is one and the same only-begotten Son, God, Word, Lord Jesus Christ, just as the prophets taught from the beginning about him, and as the Lord Jesus Christ himself instructed us, and as the creed of the fathers handed it down to us.[3]

Two Mistakes: Smashing Together or Pulling Apart the Natures

Each line of the Chalcedonian Definition is crafted with care in hopes of preserving many biblical truths about our Lord. While the whole picture is more sophisticated and historically nuanced than what we can say here, we can say in summary that the era leading up to the Council of Chalcedon saw the church beset by two problems. In relation to Jesus's two natures, one tendency was to separate the natures too much, which led to pulling the natures apart so as to split the person. The other tendency was to smash the natures together so as to lose the distinction of each nature and to create a new, third thing. Nestorianism pulled the seams of Christ's person apart and flirted with a division of the one person of Christ. Eutychianism went the opposite direction and so pressed the natures

3. "The Chalcedonian Definition," in *Creeds, Confessions, and Catechisms*, 25.

together that Christ's humanity was swallowed by his divinity or that the two smashed together to form some sort of third thing between true humanity and true divinity.

It was into this tension that the Chalcedonian Definition was written as a clarion statement. Chalcedon sought neither innovation nor novelty but fidelity to the biblical witness. While conversations about *natures* and *persons* may seem distant, overly metaphysical, and complex, it is hard to exaggerate this definition's importance. In the union of Christ's two natures in one person—the hypostatic union—lies the heart of salvation. If Christ is not truly God, he cannot save us; if Christ is not truly human, he cannot represent us. The hypostatic union is an astonishing doctrine that instructs our minds to believe that Jesus Christ is truly human and truly divine *at the same time*. Jesus really is the second person of the Trinity who came among us in flesh. The incarnation was, as John says, when "the Word became flesh" (John 1:14), and Chalcedon provides guardrails for how to articulate this wonder by affirming the biblical reality that Christ is truly human and truly divine, both natures united in one person without confusion, without change, without division, and without separation.

In the end, the Chalcedonian Definition is not inspired the way Scripture is, nor is it authoritative for believers in the same way the Bible is. Nevertheless, the conclusions from the Council of Chalcedon can keep us from swerving off the road of biblical faithfulness. The chart below illustrates how the four biblical claims about Christ are individually addressed and codified in the Chalcedonian Definition, and how each protects us from christological heresies.[4]

4. This chart is, in many ways, just another way to visualize the helpful work from Fred Sanders in his "Chalcedonian Box," which I use each semester in teaching undergraduate students. See Sanders, "Introduction to Christology," 25.

Four Biblical Claims	Chalcedonian Affirmation as Confessional Guardrails	Contra Which Heresy
1. Jesus is truly God. • John 1:1 • John 8:58 • Colossians 2:9 • Hebrews 1:3	"The same perfect in divinity" "Truly God" "Consubstantial with the Father as regards his divinity" "Begotten before the ages from the Father as regards his divinity" "Only-begotten"	Arianism (condemned at the Council of Nicaea, AD 325)
2. Jesus is truly human. • Luke 2:7 • John 1:14 • Hebrews 2:14 • 1 Timothy 2:5	"And perfect in humanity" "Truly man, of a rational soul and a body" "Consubstantial with us regards his humanity; like us in all respects except for sin" "Begotten . . . in the last days the same for us and for our salvation from Mary, the virgin God-bearer, as regards his humanity"	Apollinarianism (condemned at the Council of Constantinople I, AD 381)
3. Jesus is one person. • John 10:30 • John 14:9 • Acts 2:36 • Philippians 2:5–7	"One and the same Son, our Lord Jesus Christ" "Acknowledged in two natures which undergo . . . no division, no separation" "The property of both natures is preserved and comes together into a single person and a single subsistent being" "He is not parted or divided into two persons, but is one and the same only-begotten Son"	Nestorianism (condemned at the Council of Ephesus, AD 431)
4. Jesus has two natures. • Romans 1:3–4 • Philippians 2:6–7 • Colossians 2:9 • Hebrews 2:17	"The same perfect in divinity and perfect in humanity, the same truly God and truly man" "Acknowledged in two natures which undergo no confusion, no change" "At no point was the difference between the natures taken away through the union, but rather the property of both natures is preserved"	Eutychianism (condemned at the Council of Chalcedon, AD 451)

The Extra Calvinisticum*: Christ and His Operational Natures*

While its Latin titling gives credit to Reformation theologian John Calvin, the reality is that the doctrine of *extra Calvinisticum* was taught by early Christian thinkers such as Athanasius, Augustine, Cyril of Alexandria, and many others. However, Calvin was helpful in putting succinctly and clearly what both Scripture and centuries of Christian thinkers said before him.

The *extra Calvinisticum*, despite a rather intimidating and sometimes off-putting name, is a well of profound beauty. To put it simply, this doctrine teaches that both of Christ's natures are always active, present, and operational—at the same time—being and doing what is appropriate and belonging to that particular nature. This means Jesus's human nature and Jesus's divine nature are *always* active *at the same time* doing what is proper to both humanity and divinity. The phrase refers to the conviction that, in the incarnation, the eternal Son of God is not wholly contained within the human nature of Jesus Christ. That is to say, while the Son truly and fully assumed a human nature, he did not cease to exist beyond or outside (*extra*) that humanity. The divine nature of Christ retains its immensity and omnipresence even while united hypostatically to the finite nature of humankind. This may seem like semantics or mere theological pontification, yet before you push the doctrine to the side, consider just how marvelous the *extra* can be with two examples from Jesus's life.

First, his death. Consider Jesus hanging on the cross, that cosmic-changing scene when our Lord utters that single victorious word—*tetelestai*—"It is finished" (John 19:30). If we were to ask what exactly Jesus is doing at that moment through his two natures, the answer is marvelous. During his crucifixion, what is Jesus doing through his human nature? As simple as this may sound, he is *dying*. Christ is about to experience the death you and I deserve due to our sinfulness. Now, in that exact same moment, what is Jesus doing in his divinity? While there are a thousand things we could list here, at least one thing Jesus is doing, in that very moment when his human nature is tasting death, is "[upholding] the universe by the word of his power" (Heb. 1:3).

Do not miss this: As Roman soldiers are piercing Christ's flesh and hanging him on the tree to die a traitor's death, he is upholding the universe—*including those very soldiers*—in his divinity. By the word of his power, the divine Son is upholding the structural integrity of the very cross to which he, in his humanity, is being nailed. The nails, the cross, the soldiers—they all exist by his say-so. At any point, it would be his prerogative to cease sustaining their very life and being. These Roman soldiers think they are in charge, yet little do they know just how much the one hanging there is in control. This doctrine adds some theological weight to Jesus's words when he says, "No one takes [my life] from me, but I lay it down of my own accord" (John 10:18).

There is a similar profound beauty at the other end of Jesus's earthly life—his early days. While it may seem a bit odd, consider those fragile moments of Jesus's first few days on earth. When we think of the incarnation, we must not forget that the humanity Jesus takes on is real humanity. This means that the fragility of the first few weeks of a child's life is not lost on Christ. Like any other, this child needs sustenance. So, then, consider the intimate act between newborn and mother: Jesus nursing at Mary's breast in his early days. If we ask the same question we did when considering his death—what exactly is Jesus doing via his human nature and his divine nature *in this moment*—there is profound beauty. In his humanity, Jesus, the days-old baby, is receiving the sustenance needed to carry his life forward. Yet in his divinity, the Son, the second person of the Trinity, is sustaining the very mother who is sustaining him in his humanity.[5]

Not only does the question "What is the Son doing through his two natures?" show the beauty of this doctrine but so does "Where is the Son by virtue of his two natures?" If we continue to think of the early moments of Jesus's life in light of the *extra Calvinisticum*, we can say that while the baby in the manger is none other than the eternal Son, even in that same moment he is filling the heavens in his omnipresence. Through his humanity, he is locally present in the manger, in real space and time; through his divinity, he is omnipresent wholly everywhere without change. The doctrine upholds the mystery of the incarnation without collapsing the Creator into the creature.

We will close with what I take to be among the clearest statements from Calvin on this beautiful doctrine. He wrote, "The Son of God descended miraculously from heaven, yet without abandoning heaven; was pleased to be conceived miraculously in the Virgin's womb, to live on the earth, and hang upon the cross, and yet always filled the world as from the beginning."[6]

A Common Error in Our Day: Kenotic Christology

The doctrines of the hypostatic union and the *extra Calvinisticum* will help protect us from a common error that seems prevalent in the evangelical imagination today. This misconception says that when Christ took on flesh in the incarnation, his

5. This theological idea helps make sense of a paradoxical but beautiful sentence of poetry from Dante. In *Paradiso* 33, Dante refers to Mary as "*Vergine Madre, figlia del tuo figlio*," or "Virgin Mother, daughter of your son." We can rightly refer to Mary as the daughter of her own son without the preposterous idea that she is her own grandmother because of a mature understanding of Jesus's two natures and how they relate in one person. Jesus really is the son of Mary, as the virgin Mary is the God-bearer (*theotokos*). However, Mary really is the daughter of the Son in relation to the eternal Son's divinity, as we are all creatures who are created by the Son (Col. 1:16).

6. John Calvin, *Institutes of the Christian Religion*, trans. Henry Beveridge (Hendrickson, 2008), 2.14.4.

doing so meant that he laid aside or "took off" some of his divinity. This misguided idea is often referred to as *kenosis* or kenotic Christology. The idea is rooted in a well-intentioned but misguided reading of Philippians 2, where Paul tells the Philippian church,

> Do nothing from selfish ambition or conceit, but in humility count others more significant than yourselves. . . . Have this mind among yourselves, which is yours in Christ Jesus, who, though he was in the form of God, did not count equality with God a thing to be grasped, but *emptied himself*, by taking the form of a servant, being born in the likeness of men. And being found in human form, he humbled himself by becoming obedient to the point of death, even death on a cross. (vv. 3–8)

The reason this view is called kenotic Christology is because the word Paul uses in verse 7 for Christ "emptying" himself comes from the Greek word *kenosis*. The idea is that for Christ to take on flesh, he had to divest himself of some properties belonging to his divinity—to *empty* himself to take on flesh. Many think this emptying could consist of divine attributes or other divine prerogatives that would hinder true humanity. While preserving the true humanity of Christ is vital for a biblical understanding of Christ, attempting to preserve his true humanity by downplaying his divinity is a fatal flaw.

This means, regardless of what some (otherwise beautiful) hymns may suggest, we need not confess that "mild he lays his glory by," since Jesus, unchanging as he is, retains his glory and omnipresence via his divine nature even while he assumes flesh and takes "the form of a servant" (v. 7). Paradoxical as it is, the incarnation is a *kenosis*—or an emptying—not through subtraction but through addition. The way the second person of the Trinity "empties" himself is by assuming flesh and *taking* the form of a servant. The doctrine of the *extra Calvinisticum* helps protect us from erroneous thought by showing that Jesus could never "lay aside" his glory or attributes; he *is* his attributes, and is unchangingly so. At the same time, via the assumption of a new human nature, Jesus takes on the form of a servant and is made low for us. Affirming one is not a negation of the other, and, in fact, an affirmation of the simultaneous glory of the Son and humiliation of the Son is how we navigate all the Bible has to say about our Savior, the God-man, Jesus Christ the righteous.

Dyothelitism: Christ and the Wills of His Natures

Like the *extra Calvinisticum*, the doctrine of Dyothelitism has quite the intimidating name for those unfamiliar with theology. However, do not write off this section as overly technical, for there is much beauty in the doctrine of Dyothelitism, and I am convinced that this doctrine helps illuminate just how incredible our high priest and the work he accomplished on our behalf really are.

To begin, allow me to give a far too short but hopefully accessible definition of Dyothelitism. This doctrine teaches that Jesus Christ, after he took on flesh in the incarnation, has *two wills*—one that belongs to his divinity and one that belongs to his humanity. This simple fact saves us from a few mistakes regarding trinitarian theology and helps us read crucial passages of the Bible with a touch more accuracy.

There is a critical question at play behind this doctrine, one that might seem overly metaphysical and without much importance, but it is in fact significant. The question is this: When it comes to the notion of "will"—or what someone wants to happen, as in volition—do we locate will on the level of person or the level of nature? Again, this may seem abstract, but consider Jesus's own constitution: Jesus Christ, the second person of the Trinity enfleshed, is *one person* with *two natures*. So, if we locate will at the level of *person*, then Jesus has one will (a doctrine called Monothelitism). If we locate will at the level of *nature*, then Jesus has two wills since he has two natures, one human and one divine—the doctrine of Dyothelitism. I am convinced the latter option is quite preferable when thinking about the incarnation.

Consider the biblical scene the night before Jesus's death in which Jesus prays in agony in the garden of Gethsemane. He prays, "Father, if you are willing, remove this cup from me. Nevertheless, *not my will, but yours*, be done" (Luke 22:42). How would an interpretation of this text go if we placed the notion of will, or what Jesus wants, at the level of person? The consequence would be that this prayer is the second person of the Trinity telling the first person of the Trinity that he does not want to do his will but will surrender in the end. While this may sound innocent enough, there are some unfortunate implications of this interpretation.

For example, interpreting Jesus's prayer like this would mean that there are multiple wills in the Trinity—the Father would have his own will, the Son another will, and the Holy Spirit yet another will. If will belongs at the level of person and there are three persons in the Trinity, then the Trinity would have a multiplication of wills. However, something must enact a will, so there must be something like a separate center of consciousness as well. Moreover, enacting a will necessitates a power to operate that will, so it seems like there must be multiple powers too. Before you know it, you now have in the Trinity three wills, three powers, three centers of consciousness, and so on.

In the chapter on the Trinity, one thing I aimed to show is that the only doctrine that distinguishes the persons of the Trinity *ad intra*—or internal—is the eternal relations of origin, or how the persons eternally relate to one another as Father, Son, and Holy Spirit. The interpretation of Luke 22 above gives us several alternative ways to distinguish between the persons, and they are less than helpful. What is worse, this interpretation of Luke 22 not only predicates multiple wills in the Triune Godhead but also goes so far as to suggest that those three wills can actually disagree with one another. The Son's will in Luke 22 seems to be at odds with the Father's will. Now, of course the Son submits to the Father's will—as the perfectly obedient One in his incarnation—but nevertheless the Son seems to *want* something different from drinking the cup of God's wrath and goes so far as to request it be so.

It seems Dyothelitism offers a better interpretation. Consider how the interpretation shifts if, instead of locating will in the person, we locate will at the level of nature instead. If we make that theological move, consider the numbers at play: How many natures are in Jesus, and how many natures are in the Trinity? Well, the Trinity is *one divine nature*, and therefore the Trinity has *one divine will*—this means the Triune God is never at odds with himself since he is one (Deut. 6:4). However, Jesus, as the second person of the Trinity, while sharing in the one divine nature, in his incarnation assumes a *second* nature. This means that after his incarnation and assuming of flesh, Jesus has one will he shares with the divine Godhead—the divine will—and one will he has uniquely as one who is truly human—his human will.

When Jesus says, "Not my will but your will be done, Father," it would *not* be read, "Not the will of the second person of the Trinity but that of the first person of the Trinity be done"; instead, it would be read, "Not the will of my humanity be done, but the will of my divinity be done." Whereas one interpretation leads to some trinitarian issues, the other interpretation shows a perfect high priest, who is like us in every way according to the book of Hebrews, demonstrating what true obedience looks like—though we may want something else, our truest desire and commitment are for the will of God to be done.

Jesus's Two Wills and His True Humanity

Before we move on from the idea that Jesus has two wills—one belonging to his divine nature and one belonging to his human nature—I want to spend just a moment to show why this doctrine is not merely abstract but has immense beauty and illuminates the gospel work of Christ.

Not only does Dyothelitism protect against poor readings of passages like Luke 22, but it also illuminates just how beautiful passages like Hebrews 5 really are. Consider what the author says, paying special attention to the emphasized portions:

> In the days of his flesh, Jesus offered up prayers and supplications, with loud cries and tears, to him who was able to save him from death, and he was heard because of his reverence. Although he was a son, *he learned obedience through what he suffered*. And being made perfect, *he became the source of eternal salvation* to all who obey him, being designated by God a high priest after the order of Melchizedek. (Heb. 5:7–10)

Notice that this text gives us a time indicator: "In the days of his flesh." So, we know this text has in mind the portion of Jesus's work that occurs when he assumes flesh and dwells among us: his incarnation. It is during this era, the days of his flesh, that Jesus *learns obedience*. This phrase is astonishing. Jesus Christ, who is the second person of the Trinity now in flesh, has to *learn* to obey. The notion of Jesus needing to learn obedience is important for our discussion here because it shows that obeying the will of the Father is something *new* for the Son. The Son was not eternally obedient before his incarnation because the Son and the Father (and the Spirit) have one will. There is no need for the Son to obey or submit to the Father from all eternity because they share one essence and therefore one will. However, during Jesus's earthly life, when he takes on a new nature, and a new will with that nature, he must now learn to obey the Father.

Here is where Dyothelitism illuminates the gospel of Jesus Christ: Predicating two wills to Jesus—one will in his divine nature and one will in his human nature—protects the true humanity of Christ. If Jesus's will is truly human, it is *like ours*. Jesus's will is not automatically perfect but rather *becomes perfect*, as Hebrews says: "being made perfect" (v. 9). When we say that Jesus obtains perfection, we actually mean it. Jesus's conquering sin is not a mere show. We cannot say, "Yeah, he overcame sin, *but of course he did; he is divine*." Rather, Jesus actually procures a perfect obedience to the law of God *in his humanity*. He is really tempted, he is really obedient, he is really the One who—even in human nature—overcomes every temptation and every sin. If Jesus has only one will, and it is the will he has always had in his divinity, then this is not as astonishing of an idea. However, if Jesus, in his true humanity, overcomes Satan, sin, guilt, shame, and all their evil company, then he is the mediator who is truly like us in every way, *yet without sin*.

This idea protects and illuminates just how marvelous it is that "we do not have a high priest who is unable to sympathize with our weaknesses, but one who in every respect has been tempted as we are, yet without sin" (4:15). Jesus's humanity is like yours and mine; it is like Adam's; it is a true humanity. Yet, unlike Adam and unlike you and me, Jesus uses his true humanity—with its true human will—and is utterly perfect. This is the victory of our high priest and the majesty of his merit. He learns obedience *through suffering*—and do not miss what Hebrews says is the reward of this perfection he accrues: "Being made perfect, *he became the source of eternal salvation*" (5:9). Our salvation is predicated on this incarnate One never failing in his human nature and the will that belongs to it—he is faithful where we are fickle, he is righteous where we are rebellious, he is perfect where we are wayward. This is our Christ, the great high priest whose perfect merit becomes ours through imputation and the grace of God, who is pleased to account us perfect because of the perfection of Christ.

Delighting in the Doctrine of the Incarnation

More than in other chapters, the delight section snuck into the define section, and for good reason: it is difficult to define any element of the incarnation without our hearts erupting in delight. *God with us* is simply too good of news to wait for delight. Consequently, this section will be a touch briefer than in other chapters as we consider the wonder of the incarnation.

We should start by saying there is an obviousness to delighting in the incarnation. Without it, we are hopeless. Without it, we are still lost in our sin, still wayward and in wrong relationship with God, still strangers to the promises and covenant, still lacking the fullest revelation of God. Without the incarnation, we have not our Immanuel and still are awaiting the fulfillment of Isaiah's words: "For to us a child is born, to us a son is given" (9:6) and "Surely he has borne our griefs and carried our sorrows; yet we esteemed him stricken, smitten by God, and afflicted. But he was pierced for our transgressions; he was crushed for our iniquities; upon him was the chastisement that brought us peace, and with his wounds we are healed" (53:4–5).

Delighting in God with Us

The doctrine of the incarnation is the staggering news that God came near to us. He did not remain distant or only transcendent; he was not aloof in the halls of heaven. He clothed himself with the weakness and frailty of our flesh. The God of the cosmos saw our helpless estate and came after us. This is one of the many things that separates Christianity from other faiths in the world: While many religions call their adherents to work their way toward God in self-exaltation, Christianity brings the gospel of a God who came down through humiliation.

The wonderful title of *Immanuel*—God with us—is not an epithet of Christ to be taken lightly but the bedrock of Christian hope. When we confess that Christ is the Word who took on flesh and dwelled among us, we confess that God himself entered the particularities of human creatureliness. Like only he could, God traversed the gap between the Creator and the creature as the Creator took on the form of a servant. He knew hunger, felt fatigue, conquered temptation, endured misunderstanding, grieved at the graveside of Lazarus; he was, in every way other than sin, like us just as he was with us.

Throughout the entirety of Scripture's unfolding narrative, God graciously gives his presence to his people—from the tabernacle, to the temple, to the prophets. But these are all anticipations of something even greater: God himself dwelling among us. Jesus can say to Philip, "Whoever has seen me *has seen the Father*" (John 14:9). What we have in the incarnation is a great foretaste of the nearness of God that awaits us in the life to come. Revelation 21:3 tells us, "And I heard a loud voice from the throne saying, 'Behold, the dwelling place of God is with man. He will dwell with them, and they will be his people, and God himself will be with them as their God.'"

In the deepest places of our need, God did not send another prophet with oracles about God, an academic theologian with propositions concerning God, or a messenger that he might remain distant. In our deepest need, God gave himself in the person of Jesus Christ of Nazareth.

Delighting in God for Us

What makes God's dwelling among his people all the more beautiful is that the incarnation is not a story of *mere* nearness. It is nearness with a purpose. God is not only *with* us in Christ; God gives himself *for* us in Christ. To delight in God *for* us is to recognize that the incarnation is the opening salvo of the greatest drama in human history. This carpenter from

Nazareth—the second person of the Trinity enfleshed—lived the life we ought to have lived and suffered the death we deserved to die.

To delight in God *for* us is to consider the many ways Jesus is singularly qualified to be the great mediator between God and humankind. The solution to the plight we find ourselves in as those who have fallen in the first Adam is far beyond our greatest efforts of atonement. To delight in God *for* us is to recognize that only the One who is truly God could propitiate—or turn away—the wrath of God; only the One who is infinite could redeem our transgression against an infinite God; only the One who is eternal could ever live to make intercession for us. However, to delight in God *for* us is also to realize not only that we need God to rescue us but also that we need someone truly human to represent us. Therefore, delighting in God *for* us is recognizing that we need, in the deepest ways, one to take on the form of a servant. We need a high priest who is able to sympathize with us and is capable of fulfilling the law of God on our behalf.

Only Jesus Christ, the One who is truly God and truly human, could have been or ever will be God *for* us.

6

Justification

Delighting in Your Verdict

There are times when you are reading a book and you must stop in your tracks and simply sit with what is being said. The author may have tipped you off to something new or even reminded you of something you have always known, but the way it was said *there* deserves moments of pause and reflection. That has happened many times in my life, and one of them came as I was reading about the doctrine considered in this chapter—the doctrine of justification by faith alone.

Introducing the Doctrine of Justification

When I was a student, I came across the work of seventeenth-century theologian Francis Turretin, probably known best for his three-volume *Institutes of Elenctic Theology*. At the time, I was in a research mode, writing papers and working through the various views surrounding the doctrine of justification. When I got to Turretin, whom I had not read much at that time, he reminded me why this doctrine is so important, and his words stopped me in my tracks.

In the middle of his discourse about the doctrine of justification, Turretin reminds readers that this is no mere academic or abstract doctrine we are dealing with. With startling phrases and biblical imagery, Turretin pauses his academic articulation of the doctrine and puts things into perspective: We have sinned against a holy God. While we may intellectually affirm that notion, Turretin is worried we do not know how big of a deal this is. He is worth quoting at length here, as he brings the majesty and awe of God into our mind's eye, which puts into perspective just how beautiful the idea really is: Even though we sinned against this God, there is a way to be made right with him. Hear Turretin explain the awe-inducing severity of the Lord and how it ought to make this conversation not academic but *deeply personal*: "The controversy is not carried on coldly and unfeelingly in scholastic cloud and dust (as if from a distance), but in wrestling and agony—when the conscience is placed before God and terrified by a sense of sin and the divine justice, it seeks a way to stand in the judgment and to flee from the wrath to come."[1] He continues:

> When we come into the sight of God, it is necessary to leave such trifles because there the matter is conducted seriously and no ludicrous disputes about words are indulged. Hither our eyes must altogether be raised if we wish to inquire profitably concerning true righteousness; in what way we may answer the heavenly Judge, when he shall have called us to account. . . . When we rise to the heavenly tribunal and place before our eyes that supreme Judge (not such as our intellects of their own accord imagine, but as he is described to us in Scripture [namely, by whose brightness the stars are darkened; at whose

1. Francis Turretin, *Institutes of Elenctic Theology*, vol. 2, ed. James T. Dennison Jr., trans. George Musgrave Giger (P&R Publishing, 1992), 639.

> strength the mounts melt; by whose anger the earth is shaken; whose justice not even the angels are equal to bear; who does not make the guilty innocent; whose vengeance when once kindled penetrates even to the lowest depth of hell]) then in an instant the vain confidence of men perishes and falls and conscience is compelled . . . to deprecate the judgment and to confess that it has nothing upon which it can rely before God. And so it cries out with David, "Lord, if thou marked iniquity, who can stand?"[2]

This quote brings the proper perspective when discussing the doctrine of justification. You were once an enemy of God. So was I. Instead of walking in the way of the wise, all of us, without fail, have been summoned by the voice of lady folly and have bowed down to that which is not God (Prov. 9). Because of our status as sons and daughters of Adam together with our own sin, we were dead in our sins. Moreover, as if being spiritually dead was not bad enough, our transgressions brought not only death but also guilt. We were guilty before God. Without excuse, without any argument or reason to which we could appeal for our pardon, we stood before him.

As Turretin writes, this is the God whose brightness makes the celestial stars seem dull and dark and before whom *mountains melt*. We can only faintly imagine that day when it is our turn to stand before him. If the mountains melt, what will we do?

While this thought ought to lead Christians to tremble, we have hope. On that great and dreadful day, the doctrine of justification will be dear to us. On that day, it will be not merely a *doctrine* but our only hope. For the doctrine of justification is part of God's great plan to qualify a sinner to stand before

2. Turretin, *Institutes of Elenctic Theology*, vol. 2, 639–40. I am also grateful to Thomas Schreiner for bringing this quote back to mind as I was reading for this chapter. See Thomas Schreiner, *Faith Alone: The Doctrine of Justification* (Zondervan Academic, 2015), 16.

him, and instead of that being a day of dread, it will be the day of our supreme delight.

Allow me to return to Turretin, who shows the key to turning this dread into delight:

> When the mind is thoroughly terrified with the consciousness of sin and a sense of God's wrath, what is that thing on account of which he may be acquitted before God and be reckoned a righteous person? . . . Is it righteousness inhering in us . . . or the righteousness and obedience of Christ alone imputed to us?[3]

In this chapter, we explore the wonder that is "the righteousness and obedience of Christ alone imputed to us."

Defining the Doctrine of Justification

To work through the glory that is the doctrine of justification, I want to discuss four doctrines that all have a logical progression and relation to one another: (1) justification, (2) the active and passive obedience of Jesus Christ, (3) imputed righteousness, and (4) *sola fide*—or faith alone. The way these relate provides both the logic and the thesis of this chapter. So, let us work toward an understanding of this idea: We are *justified* before God through Jesus Christ by his *active and passive obedience* being *imputed* to us, which we take hold of through *faith alone.*

This righteousness of Christ is the basis of our righteousness, as God declares us just through the merits of his Son. To put it another way, we can be right before God because, by his grace, God has chosen to credit us with Christ's righteousness. This is not something we earn or deserve; it is freely gifted by God the Father, accomplished by the Son, and applied by the Spirit. To better understand the beauty behind this statement, it will

3. Turretin, *Institutes of Elenctic Theology*, vol. 2, 640.

prove helpful to examine those four doctrines—justification, obedience, imputation, and faith—which will also allow us to move from defining justification to delighting in the news that "Christ also suffered once for sins, the righteous for the unrighteous, that he might bring us to God" (1 Pet. 3:18).

1. Justification

Unlike other doctrines, the doctrine of justification has received substantial attention through many wonderful works, published throughout various centuries. Given the amount that has been written on the doctrine, we are not in short supply of those who have defined the term *justification*.

Recently, there have been great works published on justification that give helpful definitions. For example, Michael Horton defines justification in these words: "The view that I am defending here is that justification is simply 'the gift of righteousness.' . . . Justification cancels guilt and credits the believer with the status of Christ as righteous in the heavenly court."[4] Likewise, J. V. Fesko writes, "Justification is a judicial verdict where God declares a person in conformity with his law, and it has protological origins and is laden with eschatological significance."[5] (*Protological* is having to do with creation and the beginning, whereas *eschatological* is having to do with the end, meaning that justification is a doctrine that extends from the beginning of God's creative acts to the end of all things.)

These wonderful definitions from Horton and Fesko are helpful guides as we tour the doctrine of justification. I have also come to appreciate and find myself using the definition given by the post-Reformation theologian Petrus van Mastricht, who writes, "Justification for us is nothing other than the gracious declaration of God whereby he absolves a sinner,

4. Michael Horton, *Justification*, vol. 2 (Zondervan, 2018), 285.

5. J. V. Fesko, *The Giver of Life: The Biblical Doctrine of the Holy Spirit and Salvation* (Lexham Academic, 2024), 142.

on account of Christ's righteousness imputed to him and apprehended by him with a living faith, from the guilt of all his sins, and declares him righteous for eternal life."[6]

Van Mastricht's definition does not shy away from judicial language that suggests there is a notion of guilt being dealt with. Because of our being "in Adam" and his inability to obey in the garden of Eden, and also because of our very own sin and inability to fulfill God's law, we are guilty before a God whose holiness commands perfection, a standard we have not met—nor has anyone, for that matter (Rom. 3:23). However, though we are guilty in our sin, God has *declared*—another important word in van Mastricht's definition—that we are innocent. How can this be? How can it be that even though we have failed to follow God's law and have accumulated for ourselves a long résumé of unrighteousness, God—the holy One—has declared that we are righteous?

This question gets at the great grace and heart of the gospel of Christ. Quite possibly the best answer comes from the apostle Paul, who says, "For our sake he made him to be sin who knew no sin, so that in him we might become the righteousness of God" (2 Cor. 5:21). God did not merely sweep our unrighteousness under the rug as if to shrug his everlasting shoulders and render sin no big deal. On the contrary, the God who does not *have* holiness but *is* holiness itself would do no such thing as make light of wickedness. Far from sweeping our wickedness under a rug, God instead nailed it to a cross. The reason God can *declare* us righteous in regard to fulfilling the law is because Christ fulfilled the law on our behalf. Moreover,

6. Petrus van Mastricht, *The Application of Redemption and the Church*, Theoretical-Practical Theology, vol. 5 (Reformation Heritage Books, 2025), 170. This is quite similar to a definition from another theologian who has meant much to my thinking on justification, Louis Berkhof: "Justification is a judicial act of God, in which, he declares, on the basis of the righteousness of Jesus Christ, that all the claims of the law are satisfied with respect to the sinner." Louis Berkhof, *Systematic Theology* (Eerdmans, 1941), 513.

instead of receiving the reward for his perfect righteousness, God, who is both the *just* and the *justifier*, sees fit to credit Christ's righteousness to our account and credit our sin to his account (Rom. 3:26).

If we are in Christ, we have each participated in a cosmic trade. In the gospel, we have traded our graveclothes for the robes of Christ's righteousness. As stained by sins and marked by ruin as our graveclothes were, Christ willingly put them on and died the death our wickedness wrought. In exchange, Christ spent his days procuring a perfect righteousness through his humanity in full obedience to the law of God. By faith, we put on his robes of righteousness so that now when the Father looks at you and me, he sees the merit of his perfect Son.[7]

Returning to our definition of justification, then, it is "on account of Christ's righteousness imputed" that God can *declare*—a once and for all declaration—that we, though each a sinner, have been made right before him and can enjoy the benefits of perfect sonship. Since it is on the basis of Christ's righteousness that we enjoy the rights and privileges of being declared righteous, it is vital that we now press in to the righteousness he procured and has freely given to us by faith.

2. Christ's Active and Passive Obedience

If we search the Scriptures for the categories of Christ's *active* and *passive* obedience, we will not find those titles, per se.

7. To say that we are justified by the merit of the Son is not to diminish the work of the other two persons of the Trinity in the grace of justification. Consider, for example, the way van Mastricht demonstrates the triune reality of justification:

> The persons of the divine essence each in their own way distinctly concur in it: (1) first the Father (Rom. 8:34), by constituting, admitting, and imputing the righteousness of his Son for our justification (Rom. 8:30; 2 Cor. 5:21); (2) the Son (Isa. 53:11; Matt. 9:2, 6), by satisfying (Matt. 20:28; Eph. 5:2), and interceding as our advocate (1 John 2:1–2); (3) the Holy Spirit (1 Cor. 6:11), by testifying (Rom. 8:15), and sealing (2 Cor. 1:22; Eph. 4:30). (van Mastricht, *Application of Redemption*, 174–75)

However, we will be hard-pressed to read very far into the four Gospels without bumping into the idea rather quickly. These two categories—active and passive obedience—are helpful when trying to develop an appreciation for and an apprehension of the many ways Christ's life and work are in line with the will of God, the law of God, and Christ's identity as the Son of God. What is more, as we will come to see, for a saving righteousness that is powerful enough to not only pay for our transgression but also provide us with an unfading righteousness, both Christ's passive and his active obedience are necessary. Let us begin with a basic definition.

Active obedience is the obedience of Jesus in which he actively fulfills all the law's demands to the fullest. This obedience can be seen as we read the Gospels and see Christ actively fulfilling all that God commands by virtue of perfectly following the law. We could search the Old Testament for each command and declaration of the law, write it out, and walk through the life of Christ seeing him fulfill each iota. As Christ goes about his days, he has no wrong thought, no wrong deed, no wrong action, no wrong intuition—everything about him conforms to the high calling of God's holy law.

Passive obedience, from the Latin *passio*, is the obedience Jesus accomplishes through his suffering—such as his birth in the manger, his humiliation throughout his life, his mocking from the religious leaders, his agonizing prayer in the garden of Gethsemane, and his crucifixion. This is the kind of obedience Paul has in mind when he tells us that Christ is "obedient to the point of death, even death on a cross" (Phil. 2:8).

Both active obedience and passive obedience are tied to Christ's completely fulfilling the law of God and winning a perfect righteousness. Some of his actions are actively fulfilling the demands of the law, and some of his actions are punishment from others *for* his fulfilling the law. Or, to return to van Mastricht for a short and memorable description of both kinds of righteousness: "[The] twofold righteousness of Christ is observed, one active, whereby he kept the law exactly (Matt. 3:15; 5:17; Gal. 4:4), and the other passive, whereby he suffered for the law that we violated (Rom. 4:25; Phil. 2:8)."[8]

Now that we have a rough understanding of Christ's righteousness—procured by both his active and passive obedience to the will and law of God—we need to move on to how the righteousness achieved by Christ could possibly become *our righteousness*. For if Christ lived his life in perfect obedience to the law but that righteousness stayed outside us, it would not be the good news of the gospel; this is where the doctrine of imputed righteousness comes in.

3. Imputed Righteousness

Paul instructs the church in Philippi that the righteousness needed in Christian salvation is not self-derived but comes from outside ourselves; it is a given righteousness. Paul writes, "Not having a righteousness of my own that comes from the law, but that which comes through faith in Christ, the righteousness from God that depends on faith" (Phil. 3:9). This *given* righteousness is none other than the righteousness of Christ credited to our account. This is where the word *imputation*, which we saw in our definition of justification above, is

8. Van Mastricht, *Application of Redemption*, 174. Van Mastricht continues to show why both forms of righteousness are needed for a full understanding of Christian salvation as he writes:

> It must be maintained that the active righteousness alone is insufficient for procuring justification, because a [judgment] (*dikaiōma*) was demanded for sinners, who had earned death (Gen 2:17; Rom. 5:12; 6:23) . . . and also he did not expend on our behalf only his passive righteousness, because it is not only his passive righteousness that is referred to our salvation through Scripture (Jer. 23:6; 1 Cor. 1:30; Rom. 5:19; Phil. 3:9), but it also regards the fullness of grace that he was expended for us in the whole of what he is (Rom 8:32). Hence, both kinds of his righteousness join into our one [justification] *dikaiōma*, whereby he satisfied for the sins of those justified.

so vital. Imputation gets at the notion of *given* or *credited*. Because we have been united to Christ by faith, the righteousness of Christ has been imputed to our account. In Scripture, we can actually see *three* imputations at play that, in ways both tragic and beautiful, tell the story of our faith journey.

First, Adam's sin is imputed to us. Adam, as the representative of all humanity, fell in the garden of Eden when he and Eve ate from the forbidden tree (Gen. 3). When Adam fell, because he was our covenant representative and we were "in Adam" (Rom. 5), his sin and guilt were imputed to our account. Or, as Paul informs the church in Rome, "One trespass led to condemnation for all men" (5:18).

Second, our sin is imputed to Christ. As noted above, in the great exchange of Christian salvation, we trade our graveclothes for the robes of Christ's righteousness. When Christ takes on the sins of his people, they are placed on him so they can be crucified with him. Again, we read from Paul, this time telling the church in Corinth that God "made *him to be sin* who knew no sin" (2 Cor. 5:21).

Third, Christ's righteousness is imputed to us. The astute Bible reader will know that for both of the biblical references quoted above, the verses do not end where I cut them off. Rather, both continue into the news of God's gospel, in which neither Adam's sin nor our sin has the final word. Romans 5 continues, "Therefore, as one trespass led to condemnation for all men, *so one act of righteousness leads to justification and life for all men*. For as by the one man's disobedience the many were made sinners, so *by one man's obedience the many will be made righteous*" (vv. 18–19). And 2 Corinthians 5 continues, "For our sake he made him to be sin who knew no sin, so that *in him we might become the righteousness of God*" (v. 21).

The glory of imputation is that not only does the second person of the Trinity take on flesh, not only does he use that flesh to perfectly fulfill the letter of the law, and not only does he willingly substitute himself for the payment our transgressions called for, but he also grants us his righteousness and the cosmic inheritance found in it.

This brings us to consider one of the wonders given to us through imputed righteousness: Christ's active and passive obedience. The wonder of imputed righteousness is that the doctrine speaks a better word than mere debt cancellation. What I mean is that God has done more than just wipe away our sins and forgive our debts. He has indeed done that marvelous work, which is more than we could ever deserve, yet imputed righteousness goes even a step further. To understand this point, consider a financial example: Imagine someone has found themselves in significant debt, the kind of debt that will not only ruin them but also drag their family down and possibly sink generations. Now, imagine that someone comes up to this hypothetical person and says, "I see you, and I see the pain your debt is causing. I see that this is a situation you have no hope of overcoming, but I have good news for you. I'd like to pay off your debt completely, down to the last penny."

No doubt, this would be the cause of great rejoicing. A crippling debt now gone is a grace the person could have never imagined nor worked for on their own. However, let's also say that hypothetical debt got so terrible in the first place because the person had a severe gambling addiction and a propensity for financial mismanagement. While the debt being paid off is a severe mercy, it will pass—and if the person's account is merely brought to zero but nothing else changes, they will likely find themselves back in a significant deficit soon.

You may see where I am going with this: Sin puts each of us in a position of desperate need. We have sinned against a holy God, and our offense is far worse than we could imagine. Sin is not some small mistake worthy of a wrist slap; it is cosmic treason against the One who breathed out the stars. We each have a debt we could never pay off, and the collector is none other than the Creator of the cosmos. This is where the person and work of Christ, the righteous One, come in. While God's wrath was heading toward us like a freight train we could never derail, Christ stepped in as our propitiation and drank the wrath of God down to the dregs. Yet, he not only pays for our sins—thereby canceling our debt—but also goes a step further and grants us his own righteousness. While it would have been more mercy than we deserve for Christ to *just* cancel our sin and the record of debt held against us, if he had not also made us righteous, we would have only procured another record of debt. By his grace, he not only pays for our unrighteousness but also gives us his own righteousness. This is the glory of imputation.

To return to the financial metaphor: The imputation of Christ's active and passive obedience to our account not only gets our account out of the red, bringing us out of our infinite debt, but also goes a step further and gives us an immutable, infinite righteousness. We are not only *not* in debt; in Christ, we are unchangeably righteous. Our account is not merely paid off but infinitely full. As Michael Horton says, "It is one thing for a friend to forgive a debt and quite another to credit my account with his inheritance."[9]

4. Sola Fide–*Faith Alone*

All the beauty and wonder we have been discussing—having our record of debt canceled, having our sins paid for, the active and passive obedience of Jesus—all of this, wonderful as it is, would not be *good news* if there was not a way for us to lay claim to it. This is where the biblical and Protestant doctrine of *sola fide*—or faith alone—comes into play.

The doctrine of *sola fide* is a tutor for the contours of the Christian life. This tutor instructs us that it is nothing *in us* that brings about our justification; rather, our being *in Christ* brings

9. Horton, *Justification*, 347.

about salvation and righteousness. Given what we have said thus far about the way God has shaped Christian salvation—from justification, to Christ's twofold obedience, to imputation—it should be clear that salvation is not something we can afford on our own or something we can work to produce. As Scripture makes abundantly clear, "Salvation belongs to the Lord" (Ps. 3:8; 62:1).

It is hard to exaggerate just how much this idea is emphasized in the New Testament. What makes the new covenant *new* is that the law has been fulfilled by Christ and that righteousness can be imputed to us *through faith*, not *through works*. Faith is the instrument we use to take hold of Christ's life and work. Consider just a few passages in which this truth is explicit—that is, we do not need theological deduction or sophisticated biblical reasoning to arrive at the conclusion; the biblical authors simply say the truth plainly.

> We know that a person is not justified by works of the law but through faith in Jesus Christ, so we also have believed in Christ Jesus, in order to be justified by faith in Christ and not by works of the law, because by works of the law no one will be justified. (Gal. 2:16)

> He saved us, not because of works done by us in righteousness, but according to his own mercy, by the washing of regeneration and renewal of the Holy Spirit, whom he poured out on us richly through Jesus Christ our Savior, so that being justified by his grace we might become heirs according to the hope of eternal life. (Titus 3:5–7)

> Therefore, since we have been justified by faith, we have peace with God through our Lord Jesus Christ. (Rom. 5:1)

> Now it is evident that no one is justified before God by the law, for "the righteous shall live by faith." But the law is not of

> faith, rather "The one who does them shall live by them." Christ redeemed us from the curse of the law by becoming a curse for us—for it is written, "Cursed is everyone who is hanged on a tree"—so that in Christ Jesus the blessing of Abraham might come to the Gentiles, so that we might receive the promised Spirit through faith. (Gal. 3:11–14)

For this final passage, do not miss that the reality of faith alone is even brought forward from the Old Testament as Paul quotes Habakkuk: "Behold, his soul is puffed up; it is not upright within him, but *the righteous shall live by his faith*" (Hab. 2:4). Paul and James both do something similar as they relay the story of Abraham, arguing that even old covenant saints were saved by faith. Romans 4:3, Galatians 3:6, and James 2:23 all pull from Genesis 15:6, which reads "And he [Abraham] believed the LORD, and he counted it to him as righteousness."

These four passages are but a small taste of the many times, ways, and places the Scriptures put forward faith as the instrument by which we are saved rather than the law. Now, this is not to say the problem is with God's law—for God is holy and good; therefore, his law is holy and good. The issue is with our ability to uphold our end of the covenant by fulfilling the law. Notice that our salvation happens not through forsaking the law but through fulfillment of the law. Christ fulfills the law, and by faith we take hold of his righteous fulfillment of all God commanded.

A final point for a biblical understanding of *sola fide*, or faith alone, is that faith is the *instrument* of salvation, not itself a *work* leading to salvation. Faith being a work that saves us would undermine the very essence of salvation through faith alone. Thomas Schreiner makes this very point: "Faith saves, not because of our faith, but because of the one in whom we trust."[10] Michael Horton says similarly, "*Sola fide* is merely shorthand

10. Thomas Schreiner, *Faith Alone: The Doctrine of Justification* (Zondervan Academic, 2015), 262.

for *solo Christo*. It is not because of faith itself—its quality, intensity, or virtue—that one is justified, but because of Christ, who becomes ours through faith alone."[11] Horton continues, "Faith is not the one work on the basis of which God justifies. It is the *instrument*, not *basis* of justification. Further, while faith is a condition in the sense that only those who believe in Christ are justified, even this faith is a gift of the covenant of grace."[12]

A biblical understanding of faith's instrumentality is that it is grace that saves, while faith is how we take hold of that grace. This is why the proper way to describe Christian salvation is salvation *by* grace *through* faith. There is severe gospel hope to be had in this nuance, for if we maintain a salvation *by* grace rather than a salvation *by* faith, then Christ alone is the saving object. This means that even in seasons when our faith is frail and we are hanging on by a thread, we are no less saved than in seasons when our faith is strong and intensely confident. We are not saved by our intensity of faith; we are not saved by our confidence of faith; we are not saved by the length of our faith. On the contrary, we are saved by the *object* of our faith—which is none other than Jesus Christ, the righteous One.

Delighting in the Doctrine of Justification

Leading up to the five hundredth anniversary of the Protestant Reformation, biblical scholar Thomas Schreiner wrote on the role the doctrine of justification by faith alone played in the Reformation and how it still impacts us today. He begins his treatment of the doctrine with a needed observation: Justification by faith alone is one of God's answers to our biggest

11. Horton, *Justification*, 399.

12. Horton, *Justification*, 402. Horton continues: "God not only makes it possible to believe but actually grants faith to whomever he will. (Luke 10:22; John 1:18–19; 6:35–40, 63–65; 10:27–29; Acts 13:48; 16:14; Rom. 8:30; 9:10–24; Eph. 2:5; Jas. 1:18)" (p. 403).

problems in this life. Schreiner says, "Justification by faith alone isn't the product of rigid and brittle orthodoxy. It speaks to the minds and hearts of people all throughout history because it tackles one of the fundamental questions of our human condition: How can a person be right with God?"[13]

The Solution to Your Biggest Problem

With this question—*How can a person be right with God?*—I think Schreiner puts his finger on one of the most important questions of our days. While this may sound hyperbolic, it is not. The greatest problem you and I face is not external but internal; it is not social but deeply spiritual. Greater than our frustrations, our sufferings, our disappointments, and our anxieties is the terrifying and sobering reality that Christ is coming back to judge the living and the dead. Everyone who has ever lived will one day stand before the holy presence of our Triune God. Those who stand before the holy One cloaked in their own merit will come to know his holy presence as a terror; those who stand before the holy One cloaked in the perfection of Christ will come to know his holy presence as the deepest delight that will be their greatest treasure for all eternity.

This is our biggest problem, greater than any other we have ever faced: Apart from Christ, we are without hope. Sin is not some small blemish resolved by a cosmetic moral fix—it is an offense against the One who breathed out the stars and a rupture in the very relationship for which we were made. Left unresolved, our guilt before God will indeed lead to divine judgment and alienation from the One who is truth, beauty, and goodness. Our biggest problem, then, is not suffering, not loneliness, not anxiety, not even death itself but that we are each on a pilgrimage we cannot escape toward the presence of God—either for destruction or for delight.

13. Schreiner, *Faith Alone*, 15.

That being said, if we have clung to Christ by faith, *the number one biggest problem of our entire lives is already resolved.* That is a wild sentence. There is nothing this world can throw at us—as evil as it can be—that can remove the glorious reality that our biggest need has already been met in Christ. This is why justification by grace through faith alone is breathtakingly good news. To be justified is to have our biggest fear erased, our biggest need satisfied, and our biggest anxiety calmed; it is to have the solution our souls most need secured by God himself. Only our God would have created a path for salvation in which the judge is the justifier and the One offended is the offering. We have our biggest need met not in something *other* than God but by God himself.

We can live, then, knowing that in Christ we are secure beyond our wildest dreams. Knowing that in Christ there is nothing that can ruin the solution our souls so need. Knowing that in Christ, as Paul says, "neither death nor life, nor angels nor rulers, nor things present nor things to come, nor powers, nor height nor depth, nor anything else in all creation, will be able to separate us from the love of God in Christ Jesus our Lord" (Rom. 8:38–39).

The Death of Guilt and Shame

Like many Christians who have come before me, and likely many who will come after me, I have been beyond blessed by the church's hymnody. There are lines in the church's songs throughout the centuries that are implanted in the deepest places of my soul. The poetry and verses of these songs come up in my life for myriad reasons—to arouse joy, to soften pain, to rightsize tragedy, to help me fight temptation, to help me better see God. By God's grace, there is a song in the history of hymnody for nearly every rhythm of the Christian life.

One such verse for me comes in Charitie Lees Smith's 1863 hymn, "Before the Throne of God Above." In this hymn, Smith writes of Christ's work as our great advocate as a balm for our souls. The verse I have hidden away in my mind and heart is this one:

> When Satan tempts me to despair
> and tells me of the guilt within,
> Upward I look and see him there,
> who made an end of all my sin.[14]

Her words so capture the beauty of 1 John 2:1: "My little children, I am writing these things to you so that you may not sin. But if anyone does sin, we have an advocate with the Father, Jesus Christ the righteous."

These words—a reminder that in Christ, God is *for us*—are severely needed in our lives. It is hard to put into words just how powerful a grip shame and guilt can have on us, and, sadly, those of us who have experienced these evil twins do not need me to try to put into words what we are all too familiar with. Guilt and shame can cause us to run from the very God our souls need. Like it did with Adam and Eve in the garden of Eden, guilt grips our hearts and pervades our bodies, so instead of running *to* God, in shame we hide from his presence. What is more, because of shame and our desire to hide from God, we sew for ourselves clothes of fig leaves when before there was only unashamed freedom (Gen. 3).

Guilt and shame are merciless companions. Guilt reminds us of what we have done; shame whispers that what we have done defines who we are. Guilt follows us around replaying our failures, reminding us of words we cannot unsay and deeds we cannot undo. Shame joins the chorus, not only pointing to what we have done but also declaring who we are: broken, unworthy, unclean. These two can gnaw away at the soul and erode joy. In

14. "Before the Throne of God Above," lyrics by Charitie Lees Smith (1863). Public domain.

the deepest places of our souls, we can convince ourselves that *there is simply something about* me *that is unlovable*. Those who know me know that I fight this very thing. I have a feedback loop of self-hatred that often plays in my mind and has followed me from my earliest days. At times, it feels as though I cannot outrun it. On my worst days, it can feel as if shame is my mother and guilt is my father. As if I am the offspring of these terrors, and they have intertwined themselves in my very DNA.

Against these ruthless masters, nearly all attempts at deliverance fall short. The world's greatest therapies may provide relief for a moment, but our souls need something this world cannot offer. What our souls need is for the cosmic Judge of all to speak a better word about the crucifixion of our guilt and the death of our shame. Simply put, we need Jesus. We need him to be what only he can be and do what only he can do. As he calmed the storm the night the disciples were at sea, we need him to still the waves of our inward anguish, and, in the justifying work of his offering his life for ours, he has done just that.

In God's glorious gospel, when our souls are raging with despair and our spirits whirl within us, he rebukes the wind and raging waves. One day—even if not until we cross the Jordan—we will look at him with a mysterious awe similar to that of the disciples as they said, "What sort of man is this, that even winds and sea obey him?" (Matt. 8:27). Yes, in either this life or the next, in response to his life, death, and resurrection, there will be many praises upon our lips for our great Christ, and in the chorus of our praises will be the awe-inducing question, "What sort of man is this, that even my guilt and shame obey him?"

For some, the doctrine of justification may be a doctrinal point of war in which fights rage and applause is won. Yet, for many of us, the doctrine of justification is the warm solace of the soul and the graveyard of our guilt and shame.

7

Union with Christ

Delighting in Your Identity

God seems to be in the business of uniting parties that, on the surface, do not seem to belong together. Consider the idea of God's *uniting* work throughout the Scriptures. When God ordains the notion of marriage, he does so by uniting a man and a woman to make "one flesh" (Gen. 2:24). When Christ takes on the mission of salvation, he does so by bridging the gap between the Creator and the creature in the union of his natures both divine and human (John 1:14). Through the gospel of Christ, as the promises of God are extended to the whole world and gentiles are brought into the covenant people, God tears down the dividing wall of hostility and makes "one new man" by uniting Jews and gentiles together in the church (Eph. 2:14–3:6). If that is not enough to show God's pleasure in uniting parties that seem untenable together, consider the consummation of all things, at which time God will even unite heaven and earth (Eph. 1:10; Rev. 21:1–4).

Introducing the Doctrine of Union with Christ

Of course, all these mysterious unions are beaming with beauty, and each, in its own way, impacts us all. However, there is one more union that, for the Christian, is a deeply personal one: the union between Christ and his people. All those who have believed in Christ by faith have been united to him through the Holy Spirit, and each receives access to and justification before the Father. The Bible is replete with both direct attestation to our union with Christ and many images and metaphors that show salvation happens *in Christ*.

- We are the branches that have been grafted into and have life in the vital vine that is Christ (John 15:5–8).
- We are the many parts of the body of which Christ is the head (1 Cor. 12:12–27).
- In a "profound" mystery, the way a man is to leave his father and mother and hold fast to his wife so that the two become "one flesh" is also imagery for the reality that Christ and the church have become one (Eph. 5:28–33).
- Paul can speak of our being "baptized *into* Christ" as we "have *put on* Christ" (Gal. 3:27–28). Elsewhere, Paul can write of our having "died with Christ" and how we "live with him" (Rom. 6:8–14).

What should become clear in these passages, and many others like them, is that God has not designed Christian salvation so he can redeem us and then stay a safe distance away from us. Instead, God has designed salvation so that as we become *one with him*, we get the rewards of salvation *from him*. Christian salvation is the story of the transcendent God becoming breathtakingly near and going so far as to give himself to his people by uniting himself with them.

John Calvin famously opens the third book of his *Institutes* by writing of the hope that comes from union with Christ and how lost we would be without it: "So long as we are without Christ and separated from him, nothing which he suffered and did for the salvation of the human race is of the least benefit to us. To communicate to us the blessings which he received from the Father, he must become ours and dwell in us."[1]

Defining the Doctrine of Union with Christ

"Union with Christ" is a biblical motif when speaking of the entirety of the believer's redemption taking place *in Christ*. It goes by many names in Scripture and has many theological implications and consequences, but in its most basic form, union with Christ tells us that the gifts of salvation are not to be had apart from the Savior himself. Rather, all the gifts—election, justification, sanctification, resurrection, and more—are granted to us as we are incorporated *into* the life-giving vine that is Christ.

There are a number of theological debates related to union with Christ, but those debates are not the concern of this chapter. Rather, we will engage in a threefold explanation of union with Christ. First, I want to show how this doctrine can be right under our noses as we read the Scriptures—often hidden in those tiny words we call prepositions. Second, and building on the first point, I want to discuss how *all* Christian theology is granted through union with Christ. Finally, I want to show how even though the doctrine bears the name of the second person of the Trinity—Christ—it is a *trinitarian* doctrine that culminates in the doctrine of adoption.

1. John Calvin, *Institutes of the Christian Religion*, trans. Henry Beveridge (Hendrickson, 2008), 3.1.1.

The Gospel in Prepositions

One of my favorite lessons when introducing students to the doctrine of union with Christ is to tell them that the doctrine has been hiding in plain sight the whole time. In fact, you have likely read, reread, and memorized biblical texts that deal directly with this doctrine. Union with Christ is present throughout the Bible, and it is often hidden in the prepositions.

In case it has been a minute since you have considered grammar, prepositions are used, typically before a noun, to convey a kind of relation between two things. Prepositions can be tricky little things because they are often small words that are so common our brains do not even register to stop and consider them. For example, *at*, *by*, *for*, *from*, *on*, *to*, *with*, and *in* are all prepositions.

When it comes to the doctrine of union with Christ, we cannot afford to miss the prepositions. In these tiny words of connectivity, we can get a glimpse of the glories of God's gospel, especially as it relates to union with Christ. To show the glory found in prepositions, I often use the first fourteen verses of Ephesians to demonstrate. Take a few moments to read Ephesians 1:3–14 below and pay careful attention to when Paul uses a preposition in relation to Christ, such as "in Christ," "with Christ," "to Christ," and "by Christ." What becomes gloriously clear, using Ephesians 1 as a test case, is that much of our salvation—in fact, *all* of our salvation—is *in Christ*. I recommend you take a highlighter or pen to all the prepositions in search of what we get *in him*:

> Blessed be the God and Father of our Lord Jesus Christ, who has blessed us *in Christ* with every spiritual blessing in the heavenly places, even as he chose us *in him* before the foundation of the world, that we should be holy and blameless *before him*. In love he predestined us for adoption *to himself* as sons through Jesus Christ, according to the purpose of his will, to the praise of his

> glorious grace, with which he has blessed us *in the Beloved. In him* we have redemption through his blood, the forgiveness of our trespasses, according to the riches of his grace, which he lavished upon us, in all wisdom and insight making known to us the mystery of his will, according to his purpose, which he set forth *in Christ* as a plan for the fullness of time, to unite all things *in Christ*, things in heaven and things on earth *in him*.
>
> *In him* we have obtained an inheritance, having been predestined according to the purpose of him who works all things according to the counsel of his will, so that we who were the first to hope *in Christ* might be to the praise of his glory. *In him* you also, when you heard the word of truth, the gospel of your salvation, and believed *in him*, were sealed with the promised Holy Spirit, who is the guarantee of our inheritance until we acquire possession of it, to the praise of his glory. (Eph. 1:3–14)

I italicized only a few of the prepositional phrases in this passage in hopes of showing how we live our lives and have our faith *in him*. Consider just a few of the benefits of being united to Christ. *In Christ* we:

- get every spiritual blessing (v. 3).
- are chosen before the foundation of the world (v. 4).
- are predestined for adoption (v. 5).
- get redemption through his blood and the forgiveness of our trespasses (v. 7).
- receive revelation of the mysteries of God's will (v. 9).
- receive an inheritance (v. 11).
- are sealed with the promised Holy Spirit as the guarantee of our inheritance (vv. 13–14).

Do not miss the first item on the list: Paul makes it clear that *every spiritual blessing* is awarded in Christ, even those not in this already glorious list—yes, *every* spiritual blessing is granted us by virtue of our union with Christ. This is why it can be said without hyperbole that "union with Christ is theological shorthand for the gospel itself—a key image that pulls together numerous motifs in the biblical witness."[2]

The strategy of painting Christian salvation as union with Christ is not confined to Ephesians 1 alone. Elsewhere we see that we have lost all condemnation in Christ (Rom. 8:1), we are sanctified in Christ (1 Cor. 1:1), and we are resurrected in Christ (Col. 3:1). As Kevin DeYoung says, "Union with Christ may be the most important doctrine you've never heard of."[3] However, we can hear of this doctrine with nearly every turn of the page in the New Testament if we tune our ears to perceive the beauty and majesty of the gospel contained in prepositions—we are saved *in Christ*.

Union with Christ as the Forest of Salvation

If you spend much time reading about *soteriology*—the study of salvation—it will not take very long before you bump into a Latin phrase that has been the impetus for a lot of arguments and ink spilled. This Latin phrase is *ordo salutis*. Its definition is not too complicated, as the phrase simply means "order of salvation." The question behind this phrase is what takes place for someone to move from being a hell-bound sinner to a heaven-bound saint? Also, does it have a consistent order such that we could list what takes place in Christian salvation? For example, while Paul was not *trying* to give a sophisticated *ordo salutis* in his letter to the Romans, he provides a helpful example of one. Paul writes, "For those whom he foreknew he also predestined to be conformed to the image of his Son, in order that he might be the firstborn among many brothers.

2. Todd Billings, *Union with Christ: Reframing Theology and Ministry for the Church* (Baker Academic, 2011), 1.

3. Kevin DeYoung, *Hole in Our Holiness: Filling the Gap Between Gospel Passion and the Pursuit of Godliness* (Crossway, 2012), 94.

And those whom he predestined he also called, and those whom he called he also justified, and those whom he justified he also glorified" (8:29–30).

This becomes clearer if we break down the logical steps of Paul's words: foreknowledge → predestination → calling → justification → glorification. This God-inspired ordering of the events taking place in Christian salvation is helpful, as it seems consistent for all our stories as we follow Christ. In other words, this is not just a list in Romans 8; this is *our story*. We could use other portions of Scripture as well and add to Paul's list. While the point of this chapter is not to argue for a particular *ordo salutis*, when I teach the *ordo* in my classes, I often provide students with the following list of how I see the material ordering itself throughout Scripture:

- Foreknowledge and Predestination
- Calling
- Regeneration
- Conversion: Faith and Repentance
- Justification
- Adoption
- Sanctification and Preservation
- Glorification

While there are elements we could add to this list, it is a helpful potential ordering of what takes place in Christian salvation. Vital for this chapter is this question: Where should we place the doctrine of union with Christ in this list?

Astute readers may already see the issue based on the previous section: If the doctrine of union with Christ shows up throughout the New Testament's prepositions, showing that we are saved *in Christ*, *by Christ*, and *with Christ*, then the soteriological terrain covered by union with Christ seems greater than any *one* location in an *ordo salutis*. This is why theologians rightly say that the doctrine of union with Christ just *is* soteriology—it is not a mere step within the process of salvation. Our being united to Christ so that he and his benefits become ours *is* salvation.[4]

A quote used often when considering the doctrine of union with Christ, and for good reason, comes from the pen of John Murray in his phenomenal work *Redemption: Accomplished and Applied*. Considering the application of redemption, Murray shows how union with Christ encompasses the totality of Christian salvation:

> There is, however, a good reason why the subject of union with Christ should not be coordinated with the other phases of the application of redemption with which we have dealt. That reason is that union with Christ is in itself a very broad and embracive subject. It is not simply a step in the application of redemption; when viewed, according to the teaching of Scripture, in its broader aspects it underlies every step of the application of redemption. Union with Christ is really the central truth of the whole doctrine of salvation not only in its application but also in its once-for-all accomplishment in the finished work of Christ.[5]

Or, put another way, this time from Michael Horton: "Union with Christ . . . is the umbrella-term for the gifts (election, redemption, calling, justification, adoption, sanctification, glorification), not a substitute for any one of them."[6]

It is for this reason that union with Christ can be used as shorthand for Christian salvation. If someone is *in Christ*, all

4. For example, Fred Sanders says, "The soteriological lay of the land, I want to argue, is the domain of the doctrine of union with Christ. There is one Christian soteriology, and that is, by definition, union with Christ." Fred Sanders, *Union with Christ and the Life of Faith* (Baker Academic, 2025), 4.

5. John Murray, *Redemption: Accomplished and Applied* (Eerdmans, 1955), 171.

6. Michael Horton, *Justification*, vol. 2 (Zondervan, 2018), 347.

that belongs to the domain of soteriology belongs to them—even those elements they have yet to experience as we all await the consummation of all things. They are, nevertheless, *theirs*. In this way, it is as if "union with Christ" is the name of the forest that is Christian salvation. In this forest, there are many trees—justification, election, preservation, sanctification, adoption, glorification, and others—but these individual trees are part of the larger forest, and that forest is the doctrine of union with Christ.

Adopted by the Triune God

Among the most important truths flowing from the stream of union with Christ is the doctrine of adoption. In the doctrine of adoption, we hear the wonderful truth that God not just loves each of us but actually *likes* us. The Lord not only loves us enough to die for us but also likes us enough to bring us into his family and give us unprecedented access to himself.

Many of my students recognize that the idea of adoption is vaguely present in their Bibles, and they may even have the wherewithal to pinpoint a few key passages. But each semester I have the privilege of seeing students' eyes widen as the lights turn on, illuminating the sheer beauty of this doctrine. The Greek word *huiothesia*—adopted or adoption—is used a few times in Scripture. We see it especially as a key element in Paul's understanding of salvation as he uses the word in Romans 8:15; 8:23; 9:4; Galatians 4:5; and Ephesians 1:5.

There are other places, including within Paul's writings, where the idea of adoption seems to be in view even if the specific word is not used. For example, consider our status as sons and daughters in 2 Corinthians as Paul writes:

> I will make my dwelling among them and walk among
> them,
> and I will be their God,
> and they shall be my people.

Therefore go out from their midst,
  and be separate from them, says the Lord,
And touch no unclean thing;
  then I will welcome you,
and I will be a father to you,
  and you shall be sons and daughters to me,
says the Lord Almighty. (6:16–18)

The good news of adoption, as seen in these passages and others like them, is that we are saved not only *by* God but also *to* God. Meaning, in our union with Christ and the adoption that comes with it, we get not only the many benefits and blessings God has granted in salvation but also the ultimate prize and reward of the Christian life: God himself. Again, to use C. S. Lewis's insightful words, "The Son of God became a man to enable men to become sons of God."[7] Because we have Christ as our elder brother, we get our brother's Father as our Father (Matt. 12:49–50; Rom. 8:29; Heb. 2:11–13). So, as Lewis writes, in the Son of God, we become sons and daughters of God.

This life-altering notion is why David Garner can write, "Adoption cloaks the gospel in filial array."[8] This is a profound line and worth considering. The word *filial* gets at the idea of sonship. Christ has a *filial* relation to the Father, as he is eternally the only begotten Son who was "begotten, not made" from before all times, as the Nicene Creed says. Christ is always the eternally begotten Son of the Father, and "for us and for our salvation" the eternal Son of God becomes the temporal son of Mary. In Christ's taking on temporal sonship through the incarnation to accomplish his gospel, we are grafted into him, such that we get the otherworldly privilege of enjoying what is his—including participating in his relation with the Father.

7. C. S. Lewis, *Mere Christianity* (HarperCollins, 1980), 178.

8. David Garner, *Sons in the Son: The Riches and Reach of Adoption in Christ* (P&R, 2016), xxvi.

Even in this short paragraph, we can see how impossible it is to really consider the doctrine of adoption without considering the Triune God. This is why Fred Sanders is correct to say, "Union with Christ is a union from the Father who sends, through the Son who is sent, completed in the Holy Spirit who is from the Father and from the Son. Salvation by union with Christ is an undivided act of the Triune God."[9]

Consider both the beauty of the doctrine of adoption and the triune shape of the doctrine of adoption in Paul's words to the Galatians:

> But when the fullness of time had come, God sent forth his Son, born of a woman, born under the law, to redeem those who were under the law, so that we might receive adoption as sons. And because you are sons, God has sent the Spirit of his Son into our hearts, crying, "Abba! Father!" So you are no longer a slave, but a son, and if a son, then an heir through God. (4:4–7)

Did you catch it? Paul gives us the Trinity in eight words: "God [the first person] has sent the Spirit [the third person] of his Son [the second person]." In just eight words we get all three persons, who come up in the text not merely as a trinitarian articulation but gesture toward the doctrine of adoption. Why did God send the Spirit of his Son? The answer is adoption. God sent the Spirit of his Son *into our hearts* that we might cry, "Abba! Father!" Because we have been made one with the Son, the script of the Son has become our script! Only Jesus as the eternally begotten Son of the Father has the right to *truly* look to the first person of the Trinity and call him Father. But, in beauty incomprehensible, we have been made one with our older brother, Christ, and now the script that used to sound right only in his mouth rightly rings out from our lips, and even

9. Sanders, *Union with Christ and the Life of Faith*, 119.

we—those who were orphaned by the fall—can now say those delightful words *Abba! Father!*

Delighting in the Doctrine of Union with Christ

The streams of glory that flow from the doctrine of union with Christ are too numerous to count. It would be a life well spent giving sustained attention to the beauty that is union with Christ and the immeasurable ways this doctrine roots delight in the deepest places of our souls. If we had a thousand lifetimes, we could not survey all the splendor that is the union between Christ and his people, so a single section of a single chapter will surely be insufficient. But in hopes to bring into focus at least *some* of the wonder of union with Christ, I will treat the delights of this doctrine under two headings: the *vertical* delights of union with Christ and the *horizontal* delights of union with Christ.

Vertical Delights of Union with Christ

As for the vertical delights of this doctrine—by which I mean those delights that flow from the reality that in our union with Christ, there are benefits to be had between us and God—there are many. Paul seems to deploy a catchall phrase when considering the way our union with Christ impacts our relationship with God. In Ephesians, he writes that *in Christ* we have "every spiritual blessing" (1:3). It is as if Paul is saying, "Listen, I am going to list many, many riches you get in union with Christ, but in case I miss any, just know that *every* spiritual blessing comes from being *in him*."

As we discussed in the define section, among the preeminent gifts included in *every spiritual blessing* is the adoption we get as sons and daughters of God in the Son of God. I would like to turn back to considering adoption for a moment because there is much for us to delight in when considering not only *that* God saved us but also *how* God has designed Christian salvation.

God could have designed salvation in such a way as to keep a safe distance between himself and those he saved. Imagine that God redeems us—pays the penalty for our sin on the cross and grants us the forgiveness of our trespasses—but then tells us something like "I have paid the price for your wickedness, now stay out of my sight." Imagine that God treats us the way a reluctant stepparent treats an unwanted stepchild. When the adult enters the room, the child has to leave so as not to disturb them with their presence.

I fear that many, myself included in dark moments, see God like this. There can be a tendency to think that God saves us and kind of regrets it, as if the gospel was given with reluctance, and redemption comes with second-guessing. The doctrine of adoption is where this idea comes to an end. In the doctrine of adoption, we do not see God remaining at a convenient distance from his people in case things go poorly. Rather, we see a God who both redeems us and invites us into his home, gives us his name, lets us live in his presence, and gives us bold access to run to him whenever we would like.

We've talked about how in the doctrine of adoption we receive the script of the Son, and I would like to return to this idea of scripts and consider the script of another son in Scripture: the prodigal son, recorded in Luke 15. After the son has disgraced his father and demanded his inheritance early, he is forced to return home. However, in the parable, the prodigal son has so much shame over his actions and decisions that he tries to return home to his father not as a son but as a hired hand. While practicing what he is going to say when he sees his father, he says, "Father, I have sinned against heaven and before you. I am no longer worthy to be called your son. Treat me as one of your hired servants" (vv. 18–19).

Now consider those two precious words that become our script through the grace of adoption—a script that should have belonged to the obedient Son of God alone but becomes ours as we are made one with him. This script is seen in a few places in Scripture, including Mark 14:36, where Jesus says, "Abba, Father, all things are possible for you. Remove this cup from me. Yet not what I will, but what you will." Here, in the garden of Gethsemane, Jesus is the reversal of the prodigal son. Whereas the prodigal son utters his script after failure upon failure, sin upon sin, the Son of God utters his script after victory upon victory, in utter righteousness. These words spoken by Jesus in the garden the night before his crucifixion get to now reside on our tongues and come from our lips, for we "did not receive the spirit of slavery to fall back into fear, but [we] have received the Spirit of adoption as sons, by whom we cry, 'Abba! Father!'" (Rom. 8:15). Galatians also tells us, "and because [we] are sons, God has sent the Spirit of his Son into our hearts, crying, 'Abba! Father!'" (Gal. 4:6).

Two scripts from two sons: on the lips of the prodigal son, "I am not worthy to be called your son"; on the lips of the Son of God, "Abba! Father!"

The first is the script of a rejected son with his head held low. The words of one who has wasted his days among the pigs and has no hope for the future. This is the script of one who is clothed in guilt, embarrassment, and shame in the presence of his Father.

The second is the script that deserves an exclamation point! It is the shriek of the joyful child who knows that in the presence of their Father are pleasures forevermore. This is the script of one who needs not even say much—two words suffice: *Abba! Father!* There is no need for the proliferation of words because in just these two—our Father—is the proliferation of joy.

Now, do not miss this: Through our union with Jesus Christ, he has become our elder brother and shares with us all things, including his obedience, his righteousness, his inheritance, and eventually even his reign over the cosmos. However, the glory does not stop there. In our union with our elder brother—Jesus Christ—he also shares his script with us because he shares his relationship to the Father with us. In our union with Christ, what was once our script—the words of the prodigal son, "I am not worthy to be called your son"—is brought to an end. The unworthiness has been resurrected to worthiness, not because of something wrought in us but because of the worthiness of our great high priest, Jesus Christ the righteous One. So, with our elder brother, instead of hiding from God in shame and recounting our guilt before him, we, with abandonment of any other hope, *run* to him, like a child runs to their good father, with a shriek of words we do not deserve to utter but now get to utter in Christ: "Abba! Father!"

To delight in the doctrine of union with Christ is to delight in the fact that God has *you*, and—more shocking—you have *him*. You have a new identity as a son or daughter of the good Father. Your identity is wrapped up in Christ and is as sure to stand as Christ is sure to stand. Union with Christ resurrects a new identity for each of us, one that leads to deep delight. I end this section, then, with the great words of Rankin Wilbourne, who has written a wonderful book on the doctrine of union with Christ:

> If you are in Christ, your life and your story become enfolded by another story, Another's story. You don't have to discover or craft, create or achieve, invent or reinvent your own identity. Your identity is found not deep within yourself but *outside* of yourself. Your self-understanding becomes inseparable from who God says you are in Christ.[10]

10. Rankin Wilbourne, *Union with Christ: The Way to Know and Enjoy God* (David C. Cook, 2018), 145.

Horizontal Delight of Union with Christ

The beauty of union with Christ does not terminate in the vertical plane; it spills over into the horizontal, knitting together the community of the redeemed. To be united to Christ is simultaneously to be united to all who belong to him. This renders the church not some voluntary club, bound by mere preference or culture, but a mystical body joined together in its head: Christ himself. Union with Christ is the death of overly individualistic spirituality as we recognize, by God's overwhelming grace, that there are many other branches grafted into this life-giving vine. It is also the death of community based on mere commonality. What I mean is that the church—the community of saints—is not held together by ethnicity, hobbies, interests, proclivities, or any weak threads that break as differences arise. As Paul writes, "So we, though many, are one body in Christ, and individually members one of another" (Rom. 12:5), and in this one body "there is neither Jew nor Greek, there is neither slave nor free, there is no male and female, for you are all one in Christ Jesus" (Gal. 3:28).

The bond uniting Christians to one another is profoundly strong. Unlike earthly communities, whose members gravitate toward one another over common interests like sports teams, geographical locations, hobbies of interest, and the like, what brings this community together is the stronger connection of having our deepest needs met in the person and work of Christ as we are united to him in his life, death, and resurrection.

Christ's declaration that "I am the vine; you are the branches. Whoever abides in me and I in him, he it is that bears much fruit, for apart from me you can do nothing" (John 15:5) means that there is an ethic flowing from the vital vine into the lives of the branches—an ethic of the kingdom of God. This ethic is marked by virtues such as love, joy, peace, patience, kindness, goodness, faithfulness, gentleness, and self-control, and, in love, this is how we will live with the other branches as we pilgrimage together. In Christ we forgive "as God in Christ forgave you" (Eph. 4:32). In Christ we "bear one another's burdens, and so fulfill the law of Christ" (Gal. 6:2).

There is both good and bad news here at the end of this chapter on union with Christ. The bad news is that this chapter is woefully insufficient at numbering the multitude of blessings that flow from this doctrine. The good news is that such a task—writing out the fullness of delight that is union with Christ—would be a fool's errand anyway. As the apostle John reminds us, "Now there are also many other things that Jesus did. Were every one of them to be written, I suppose that the world itself could not contain the books that would be written" (John 21:25). The good news of union with Christ—the One who did such work that no book could contain it—has become *ours* through the Spirit's breathtaking work of uniting us to Christ.

To end, and in sum of much that has been said about this glorious doctrine, perhaps what is most beautiful to me about the doctrine of union with Christ is that it keeps together the wonderful gifts of salvation and our preeminent treasure: the Savior himself.

8

Preservation

Delighting in Your Security

Those who have been united with Christ through faith need not spend their days worrying if their salvation will remain secure. There is a deep well of security in God's work of redeeming a wayward people—and, to put it simply, *he has us*. I hope your takeaway from this chapter, by the time you reach the end, is that the Christian life is not a tightrope walk across a canyon of condemnation but a pilgrimage under the shelter of divine protection and provision.

Introducing the Doctrine of Preservation

However, I should start with a confession: Of all the chapters in this book, this may have been the hardest for me to write. Not because the doctrine is overly difficult or because of some intellectual conundrum that arises from sustained attention to the doctrine of preservation, but because while I intellectually believe in this doctrine and am convinced it is faithful to the biblical text, I often do not *feel* it.

I suffer from an inner voice that is less than kind. It is not hard for me to get to a place where the things I say to myself or believe about myself are antithetical to the gospel of grace. Now, it is no challenge for me to believe the gospel on behalf of others. I am convinced that no one is beyond the gospel; the good news is that Christ's life, death, and resurrection can redeem *anyone* regardless of how broken their past is. What is difficult for me is to believe the gospel can redeem *me*. Despite what I know to be true biblically and theologically, I have an inner feedback loop that can tell me I am too dirty for the gospel, too inconsistent to be loved, too frail for God to not have regrets about saving me. Moreover, even if I can get to a place where I begin to believe the gospel is not just good news for the whole world but good news even for Ronni Kurtz, it is another step to believe that I am *secure* in that gospel.

What I have learned, after years of pastoral ministry and teaching theology, is that I am not alone in this. I have spent innumerable hours counseling church members and discipling students about this very issue. There seems to be a low-grade hum in the back of many evangelicals' minds that speaks a word of insecurity regarding salvation. In the wake of spending so many hours thinking and writing about the security of believers in the hands of God, I pray that this doctrine moves its way from the pages of Scripture into the deepest places of our souls—those places where insecurity lingers. I pray we can trade our inner self-condemnation for a security in not only who God has made us to be but also his love and covenant faithfulness toward us.

While not a silver bullet in the battle against lack of security, I am convinced that prolonged contemplation on the doctrine of preservation will bolster our souls' ability to believe that God not only has saved us but also will keep us. There is much to consider when thinking through a doctrine like the preservation of God's people—yet one unmistakable move that should come with sustained attention to God's preserving powers is an upward movement of our eyes. We should take our minds off our being unworthy, frail, or unlovely and gaze upon that surety that comes from him being worthy, faithful, and the One whose very essence is love (1 John 4:7).

Defining the Doctrine of Preservation

The good news concerning the doctrine of preservation is that even when we do not *feel* like we are secure, our assurance remains untainted. The doctrine of preservation of the saints is a lifeline for weary pilgrims pressing on toward glory. Preservation shows us that the God who saves us is the God who keeps us, and our future is not suspended on the thin thread of human resolve but fastened by the unbreakable cords of divine grace and mercy. In a world of instability and frailty, the preservation of the saints anchors our souls in the unchanging character of God and the unbreakable promises of his Word.

To define the doctrine of preservation, I want to proceed with two sections. First, I want to consider the difference between the notions of "preservation of the saints" and "perseverance of the saints," showing the relationship between the two ideas and why we need *both* for a biblically faithful understanding of Christian security. Second, for much of this chapter, I want to develop a sevenfold argument for why we should hold to the security of believers as stated in the doctrine of preservation.

My hope is that these seven lines of reasoning will together form a rich and resilient tapestry of assurance. We will reflect on (1) God's immutable decree, (2) the logic of "the golden chain of redemption," (3) Christ's success in his saving mission, (4) the ongoing and efficacious intercession of Christ, (5) our union with Christ, (6) the Holy Spirit as our seal and guarantee of redemption, and finally, (7) the inseparable work of the Trinity. Each of these threads—woven through the fabric of Scripture—testifies to the same glorious reality: Those whom God has redeemed he will surely keep.

Preservation Versus Perseverance

First, a helpful distinction to make when discussing the security of salvation is the difference in definition and emphasis between "preservation of the saints" and "perseverance of the saints." You will hear Christians refer to this doctrine by both names, and in rare cases, you may even hear Christians argue that one is true and not the other.

When teaching the doctrine of assurance, I like to show students why *both* of these names for the doctrine are true and needed and why they are not mutually exclusive. Rather, they are a double stream that flows into the ocean of Christian assurance of salvation. Even considering the variance of the two words can reveal the difference between them. For each title, where is the emphasis—God or believers? For *preservation*, the emphasis seems to be on God as the One who is *preserving* Christians and making sure they make it until the end. For *perseverance*, the emphasis seems to be on believers themselves enduring until the end.

I am convinced, when turning to the biblical data, that *both* emphases are in Scripture and are needed. Sanctification in the Christian life is both an act of God *and* an act of believers. In various places in Scripture, we can see that we are active in the task of perseverance. Writing to the Colossians, Paul says, "And you, who once were alienated and hostile in mind, doing evil deeds, he has now reconciled in his body of flesh by his death, in order to present you holy and blameless and above reproach before him" (1:21–22). Then he gives a significant "if": "*if* indeed you continue in the faith, stable and steadfast, not shifting from the hope of the gospel that you heard" (v. 23).

This kind of call for Christians to endure to the end, to finish well and keep going, is seen in many New Testament passages. Consider these few as just a sampling:

> You will be hated by all for my name's sake. But the one who endures to the end will be saved. (Matt. 10:22)

> For we have come to share in Christ, if indeed we hold our original confidence firm to the end. (Heb. 3:14)

> For you have need of endurance, so that when you have done the will of God you may receive what is promised. (Heb. 10:36)

> Blessed is the man who remains steadfast under trial, for when he has stood the test he will receive the crown of life. (James 1:12)

> Therefore, brothers, be all the more diligent to confirm your calling and election, for if you practice these qualities you will never fall. (2 Pet. 1:10)

These verses, and many like them, come together to give the Christian an unmistakable charge: *Keep going*. We are called to hold fast and to "watch [our] life and doctrine closely" (1 Tim. 4:16 NIV). We are called to consistency and steadfastness as we pilgrimage through this life, marching toward the promised land.

And yet, with all these passages calling the Christian to endure, we know that this kind of perseverance is possible only because—at the same time—God is preserving us. In fact, while I believe that both perseverance and preservation are called for in a robust Christian understanding of assurance, these two have an *asymmetrical* relationship. What I mean is that while Christians are called to endurance and perseverance, I believe, in the end, the *primary* reason we can have hope that we will cross the Jordan and can be assured we'll make it till the end is because God is faithful to his Word and his work. He will see our salvation through to the end.

As we did with perseverance, consider these few passages that show the other side of the coin of assurance: that *God* is the one preserving Christians, even as we ourselves persevere.

> All the Father gives me will come to me, and whoever comes to me I will never cast out. . . . I should lose nothing of all that he has given me. (John 6:37, 39)

> My sheep hear my voice, and I know them, and they follow me. I give them eternal life, and they will never perish, and no one will snatch them out of my hand. (John 10:27–28)

> So that you are not lacking in any gift, as you wait for the revealing of our Lord Jesus Christ, who will sustain you to the end, guiltless in the day of our Lord Jesus Christ. (1 Cor. 1:7–8)

> Now may the God of peace himself sanctify you completely, and may your whole spirit and soul and body be kept blameless at the coming of our Lord Jesus Christ. He who calls you is faithful; he will surely do it. (1 Thess. 5:23–24)

> Now to him who is able to keep you from stumbling and to present you blameless before the presence of his glory with great joy. (Jude 24)

These two groups of biblical passages come together to demonstrate what Paul says so succinctly in Philippians 2: "Work out your own salvation with fear and trembling, for it is God who works in you" (vv. 12–13). Perseverance is seen in the imperative to work out our salvation, and preservation is seen in the indicative that it is God who works in us. These double truths ought to develop your confidence that even until the end of all things, you, Christian, will remain.

Seven Arguments for Preservation

Now that we have the distinction between and the significance of perseverance and preservation in our minds, we can proceed toward developing seven arguments or lines of reasoning for affirming the preservation of the saints. As I tell my students, maybe none of the seven arguments *in itself* is singularly convincing; the hope is that taken together, these seven lines of reasoning present a strong case to your own soul that your God will preserve you until the end. When this life is said and done, he has you, and you will be with him forever.

1. God's Immutable Decree

At the foundation of Christian assurance lies the unchanging will of God. His decree—eternal, wise, and immutable—is not subject to revision or reversal. The book of Numbers declares, "God is not man, that he should lie, or a son of man, that he should change his mind. Has he said, and will he not do it? Or has he spoken, and will he not fulfill it?" (23:19). These questions should be answered with a resounding *no*. God will not go back on his promises; God will not fail to come through on his Word. All God has decreed will come to pass, and if God has decreed our salvation in election, he *will* see it through.

In Malachi, God says, "For I the Lord do not change; therefore you, O children of Jacob, are not consumed" (3:6). If we have been united to Christ in the new covenant, we are counted among the "children of Jacob." There is a security rooted in God's unchangingness that ought to overwhelm all doubt or restlessness.

Often, Christians turn the doctrine of election into a matter of debate and division. It should not be so. Instead, God's declaration of salvation ought to be a well of joy and assurance—the unchanging One has spoken an unchanging word about an unchanging salvation. The unchanging God has taken on flesh in the second person of the Trinity and has procured an unchanging righteousness. The unchanging Spirit in the third person of the Trinity is our unchanging seal and guarantee that God's unchanging will, in the end, will deliver each of us into the unchanging glory of his unchanging kingdom. God has spoken, and he will do it. He has said it, and it will come to pass.

2. The Golden Chain of Redemption

Readers may have heard of "the golden chain of redemption," a phrase that refers to the list of salvific events in Romans 8:29–30, which we mentioned in our discussion of *ordo salutis*. Paul writes:

> For those whom he foreknew he also predestined to be conformed to the image of his Son, in order that he might be the firstborn among many brothers. And those whom he predestined he also called, and those whom he called he also justified, and those whom he justified he also glorified.

While not an exhaustive list of all that takes place in the process of Christian salvation, this passage shows many treasures Christians receive in Christ. We are foreknown, predestined, called, justified, and glorified. What is easy to miss, however, is that there seems to be a one-to-one correlation between those items at the beginning of the list and those at the end. To put it another way: There are no breaks in the golden chain of redemption.

The text *does not* say, "*Most* who are foreknown will also be predestined; a *majority* of the predestined will also be called. About *half* of the called will be justified. A *handful* of the justified will make it to glory." On the contrary, there is profound beauty in Paul's use of "those." *Those* foreknown are predestined. *Those* predestined are called. *Those* called are justified. *Those* justified are glorified. By God's grace, if we have experienced one, we will experience all. For our purposes in this section: If we have been justified by faith, we *will* be glorified, as God will preserve us until the end. If Romans 8 can be accurately called "the golden chain of redemption," we know that by the power and work of God, who is unchanging in all his ways, no link in this chain is in danger of breaking.

We can know this application of assurance is an appropriate takeaway from the golden chain of redemption, as Paul goes on to ask a series of vital rhetorical questions: "What then shall we say to these things? If God is for us, who can be against us? . . . Who shall bring any charge against God's elect? It is God who justifies. Who is to condemn?" (vv. 31–34). Paul wants his readers to *feel* the answer to these questions: *no one*. He concludes this series with one final, penetrating rhetorical question: "Who shall separate us from the love of Christ? Shall tribulation, or distress, or persecution, or famine, or nakedness, or danger, or sword?" (v. 35). His answer should ground a profound assurance in the deepest places of our souls:

> No, in all these things we are more than conquerors through him who loved us. For I am sure that neither death nor life, nor angels nor rulers, nor things present nor things to come, nor powers, nor height nor depth, nor anything else in all creation, will be able to separate us from the love of God in Christ Jesus our Lord. (vv. 37–39)

3. Christ's Perfect Work

Of all seven arguments for preservation of the saints in this chapter, perhaps none impacts me quite like considering Jesus's words in John 6. I recall studying this doctrine in college, not for any assignment but for my own inward turmoil. As I mentioned, I did not *feel* secure in my salvation and doubted any doctrine that told me otherwise. John's Gospel came and pierced my doubting heart like a grace-laced dagger.

John 6 chronicles a back-and-forth dispute between Jesus and the Jewish leaders. Jesus's famous words "I am the bread of life" (v. 35) cause the leaders to grumble. In Jesus's explanation about what it means for him to be the bread of life and how those who eat of his flesh and drink of his blood will never again hunger and thirst, he states the purpose for which he came down from heaven. Jesus says, "All that the Father gives me will come to me, and whoever comes to me I will never cast out. For I have come down from heaven, not to do my own will but the will of him who sent me" (vv. 37–38). We know, this side of revelation, that Jesus is referring to the Father—his incarnate mission is to accomplish the will of the Father, who sent him. The vital question, then, is what is the will of the Father for the Son's mission on earth?

This is Jesus's answer: "And this is the will of him who sent me, that I should lose nothing of all that he has given me, but raise it up on the last day. For this is the will of my Father, that everyone who looks on the Son and believes in him should have eternal life, and I will raise him up on the last day" (vv. 39–40).

The logic here is important, so I want to make it clear: Jesus says he has come to do the Father's will; the Father's will is that *none* who believe in Jesus should perish but that *all* of them will be raised on the last day. It is not too large a leap to argue that if Jesus was perfect in fulfilling the mission for which he was sent, then none of those who believe upon Christ will be lost. Indeed, they all will be raised on that final great day.

Moreover, there are only three candidates who could plausibly cause someone to "lose" their salvation—God, a third party, or oneself. I am convinced that John 6–10 eliminates any of those potential impetuses for the loss of salvation. Consider each of the three options. First, as for God, Jesus says in John

6:37 that he—God—will never cast us out, so this first option is not possible. Second, as for a third party, Jesus says, "My sheep hear my voice, and I know them, and they follow me. I give them eternal life, and they will never perish, and *no one will snatch them out of my hand*. My Father, who has given them to me, is greater than all, and *no one is able to snatch them out of the Father's hand*" (10:27–29). Third, and finally, as for oneself, we have no reason to think that we are not counted among those who are not powerful enough to snatch someone, even ourselves, out of God's hand in John 10. Moreover, given John 6, we have every reason to believe that *all* who believe *will* receive eternal life—especially when considering the remaining six arguments. It seems that due to the Triune God's saving work in the economy of redemption, there is no party outside of God powerful enough to snatch his people from him. And God in himself, due to the plenitude of his own life and grace, will never cast us off. Therefore, we answer Paul's rhetorical question, "What will separate us from the love of God?" with an emphatic *no one and nothing*.

4. Christ's Efficacious Intercession

In the heavenly court, Christ the righteous stands as the Christian's eternal advocate. Scripture tells us that after his ascension, the Son "always lives to make intercession for them" and consequently that "he is able to save to the uttermost those who draw near to God through him" (Heb. 7:25). Christ's intercession is not a mere gesture of goodwill; it is the invincible declaration that his atoning work is enough to save Christians "to the uttermost."

As in the previous point, Romans 8 proves important, as the intercession of Christ operates in the space between the *already* and the *not yet* of Christian salvation (more on this in chapter 10). We know, as those who have put our faith in Christ, that we are justified *now*, and we also know that we are still awaiting the full reception of that salvation. Our days are in the crosshairs of being *already* saved but *not yet* seeing it fully concluded. It is in this gap in which Christ anchors us through his intercession. As Paul writes, "Who is to condemn? Christ Jesus is the one who died—more than that, who was raised—*who is at the right hand of God, who indeed is interceding for us*" (v. 34).

It is easy to forget that we truly have a high priest in Christ, One who is greater than all the priests who came before him. Our assurance rests not on fluctuating faithfulness found in ourselves but on the merit of our high priest. The resurrected and ascended Christ is right now pleading our case—through his own merit and his spilled blood—and in that intercession there is an eternal well of assurance for the Christian today. The intercession of Christ, and all his high priestly work, is the theological truth behind these words from John: "If anyone does sin, we have an advocate with the Father, Jesus Christ the righteous" (1 John 2:1). In sum, Christ is praying for each of us, and Christ's prayers work.

5. Union with Christ

Writing to the church in Colossae, Paul says, "For you have died, and your life is hidden with Christ in God" (Col. 3:3). That notion of being "hidden in God" describes the doctrine of union with Christ. This doctrine received an entire chapter's worth of attention already, and for good reason—it is simply among the most profound, life-altering, and beautiful doctrines in the Christian faith.

As we saw in chapter 7, among the many implications flowing from the doctrine of union with Christ is the security of believers. When God sets out on the business of saving sinners, his way of doing so is remarkably *personal*. God does not save sinners only to put as much distance between them and himself as possible; rather, God saves sinners by uniting them to Christ—such that we are *in him*. Jesus himself says, "I am the vine; you are the branches" (John 15:5). Our salvation is one of being grafted into the vine of Christ, and we, as branches, derive our life from the vitality of the vine. If the vine goes under, so do the branches. If the vine dies, so do the branches. But as the vine has life, so, too, will the branches.

The way this unity flows into assurance is staggering. It is not a stretch to say that *as sure as* the vine is to live, *so, too*, are the branches. This means that as secure as Christ is, so, too, are those united to him. Another biblical metaphor is that Christ is the head of the body and we are the parts (1 Cor. 12:12–27). Similar to the vine metaphor, as sure as the head is to remain full of life, so, too, is the body.

All this to say: If we are sure Christ will make it to the end, you and I can be that sure that we, who are united to him, will also make it to the end. Since our salvation is *in him*, we will go where he goes. There are few greater points of assurance than this: Our spiritual lives are not exposed to decay or liable to be lost, since they are enfolded into the resurrected life of the Son. If Christ will not be cast out, neither will those who are united to him. If Christ cannot be lost, neither can you and I. If Christ stands, we stand.

6. The Spirit as Our Guarantee

Among the numerous gifts bestowed upon us in God's redemption, the most significant is the gift of God himself. One way this wonder shows up is that the Holy Spirit indwells believers (John 14:15–17; Rom. 8:9; 1 Cor. 6:19). There is another book's length of material concerning the beauty that is the indwelling work of the Holy Spirit, but one aspect of the Spirit's indwelling presence I want to be sure to mention is one that is often forgotten or overlooked. That is this: The Spirit's presence within each believer is not passive; rather, he is the living assurance of our future inheritance. The Spirit is the *guarantee* that all God's promises in his economy of redemption *will* come true for those who have the Spirit.

Do not miss Paul's words in the opening chapter of Ephesians: "When you heard the word of truth, the gospel of your salvation, and believed in him, [you] were *sealed with the promised Holy Spirit, who is the guarantee of our inheritance until we acquire possession of it*" (1:13–14). The beauty in the way God has ordained salvation is that the inheritance should not be in doubt, as the guarantor is God himself—the Holy Spirit. If we are in Christ, we have already experienced many gifts that come along with redemption: being united to Christ, being forgiven, the removal of God's wrath, being adopted into God's family, and much more. The indwelling presence of the Holy Spirit is the guarantee that all you and I *have yet* to experience will indeed come; as sure as there are breath in our lungs and blood in our veins, we are as sure to inherit all God has promised. The Spirit guarantees it. As Paul writes, we *know* and have complete confidence that "all the promises of God find their Yes in him. That is why it is through him that we utter our Amen to God for his glory. And it is God who establishes us with you in Christ, and has anointed us, and who has also *put his seal on us and given us his Spirit in our hearts as a guarantee*" (2 Cor. 1:20–22).

If you and I have the Spirit, our salvation *will* be brought to completion; we can rest assured that our inheritance is coming.

7. The Inseparable Work of the Trinity

Of all seven lines of reasoning for the doctrine of preservation, this one may be the most abstract or theologically involved. To understand the argument fully, we must know another doctrine within trinitarian theology, the doctrine of *inseparable operations*. In its most basic form, inseparable operations is a doctrine that says the Trinity acts inseparably. Since the three persons of the Trinity—Father, Son, and Holy Spirit—are one in essence, they are one in will. Since they are one in will, they are one in operation. It is not the case that the persons of the Trinity all possess their own will and consistently have to get on the same page with one another about what they want to achieve. Rather, the persons share a single divine will and act in a single divine operation. (Now, of course, as we discussed earlier, Jesus takes on a second will when he assumes a human nature in the incarnation; this is why he can say, "Not my will, but yours, be done" in the garden of Gethsemane [Luke 22:42].)

Since the persons of the Trinity act inseparably, we can expect their appropriated work in the economy of redemption to be inseparable. To put it another way, there will not be disagreement between the work of the Father, the Son, and the Holy Spirit as they set about the business of redeeming a sinful people. The way inseparable operations impacts the doctrine of assurance may not be obvious, but at least *one* implication of inseparable operations seems to be that those whom the Father elects, those whom Christ redeems, and those whom the Spirit seals ought to be the same. The Father will not elect a people for himself just for the Son to redeem a separate people; the Son will not accomplish redemption for a people just for the Spirit to apply his work to a separate people. So, then, a line of reasoning similar to that of the golden chain of redemption might sound something like this: All those whom the Father predestined the Son has redeemed, and all those whom the Son has redeemed the Spirit has sealed and guaranteed.

Delighting in the Doctrine of Preservation

Since we have been considering seven "arguments" for the doctrine of preservation of the saints, it is important to point out that this is not a doctrine that lives in theological books or academic classrooms to be merely *argued*. Rather, the doctrine of preservation of the saints is a doctrine for the pew, for the hospital bed, for desperate prayers, and for the dark nights of the soul. God's preserving faithfulness ought to be a balm for the weary and life-giving in days of suffering.

In fact, the leap from defining the doctrine to delighting in the doctrine is perhaps smallest in this chapter on preservation and assurance. The reasons for our souls to delight in God's preserving work in our lives ought to be obvious, but they are still worth expounding that we may revel in his grace toward us. While there are many worthy reasons to delight in the doctrine of preservation, I want to talk about a few that fit under two headings: rest and repentance.

Rest in Light of Preservation

Augustine's famous line from his *Confessions*—"Our hearts are restless until they rest in you"—has echoed across the centuries because it diagnoses the human condition with a physician's precision.[1] Beyond how precise and beautiful this quote from the African theologian is, it is interesting to note that Augustine wrote those words in roughly AD 400. This means, if you resonate with the notion of a restless heart, it is not a new phenomenon. We as a people are restless, and we have been restless for a *long* time.

We can talk about the notion of restlessness in a few ways, one that seems more tragic than the other. The first is the way that Augustine suggests—a restlessness with all this world has to offer and one that will find a solution only in resting in God. Like a compass needle that quivers until it finds its north, our desires, fears, and loves rattle inside us and find no steadiness among created things. This should not surprise us. Peter calls the church the "elect exiles" in 1 Peter 1, which rightly identifies our existence as that of exiles—we are *not home* here. On this side

1. Augustine, *Confessions*, trans. Henry Chadwick (Oxford University Press, 1991), 3.

of the Jordan and this side of the resurrection, the lesser beauties of this earth can only point us toward the truly beautiful One. Augustine is correct, then; as exiled pilgrims in a land that is not our home, we will never find rest until we rest in the Lord.

However, there is another way we can talk about restlessness, and I believe it is more tragic than—and maybe just as pervasive as—Augustine's. For many of us who would agree with him—"Yes, our hearts will indeed remain restless until we come to the Lord for our true rest"—we also feel restless even *after* we have begun our resting in God. This is a restlessness of the soul, an inner tossing and turning, which can sound quite antigospel. It is the inner voice of those of us who, while we have already placed our trust in the Lord and cling to Christ by faith, still have the spiritual posture of looking over our shoulders in guilt and shame.

This inward restlessness comes in many forms. Maybe it is a subtle self-doubt that we could really be redeemed. Maybe we have a flood of questions about if we have "done enough" in life. Maybe we have a low hum that slightly rings in our ears, saying, "Sure, God may love me enough to die for me, but that does not mean he actually *likes* me." Maybe we have a belief that the gospel is good news for other people but a difficulty believing that the life, death, and resurrection speak a better word about our *own* lives. There are many ways to still have a restlessness of soul even after starting the process of resting in God. But do not miss this: Even our restlessness and weariness of soul take place in the rest of Christ.

What I mean by this is that any restlessness of soul we may feel does not put us outside the rest that belongs to the Lord. We may *feel* restless as the gospel continues finding its way into the deepest places of our souls, but even as this transformation takes place—in its victories and in its failures—*he has us*. Like the author of Hebrews tells us, unlike Moses, Jesus is the kind of leader and Lord who will *actually* deliver us into rest. Unlike

Joshua, Jesus is the kind of leader and Lord who will actually deliver us into a rest that is *eternal* (Heb. 3:16–19; 4:8–13). We can strive toward realizing the rest found in God in this life while knowing our rest in the next life is assured—not by us but by him who holds us.

I started this chapter with a confession: I do not often *feel* the doctrine of preservation. I often live with an inner feedback loop in my head recounting my worst moments and becoming my worst critic. It is hard to rest when the inner voice of accusation rouses in our minds. It is hard to rest when we place ourselves in the seat of judge, and all the evidence goes in favor of our guilt. It is hard to rest when there is turmoil and chaos both "out there" and raging loudly "in here." However, I once heard a pastor say that in Christ even the joylessness we often feel is a forgiven joylessness.[2] I would add to that here: Even the restlessness we feel is a forgiven restlessness. Moreover, Christ's ability to rest in God perfectly and fully is imputed to us by faith.

Therefore, while we may not *feel* rest, the reality is that our resting is not contained in how much we feel it. Rather, our rest comes from the rest Christ has already won and purchased for us. There is a rest in preservation that nothing in this world can touch. We can go to bed tonight confident that in the morning we will wake up still a Christian because God, through the wonderful work of the gospel of Christ, has hold of each of us and will not let us go.

Repentance in Light of Preservation

When I set out to write this chapter, there was an intimidation that came with writing the delight section. I know how

2. I tried hard to find the source of this wonderful idea. My memory tells me it is a quote from John Piper, but I could not find an original source. The closest I found was Piper's wonderful response in his *Ask Pastor John* podcast, episode 1,339, "Does Christ's Righteousness Cover My Joylessness?," May 6, 2019, www.desiringgod.org/interviews/does-christs-righteousness-cover-my-joylessness.

badly my own soul needs the assurance that comes from the doctrine of preservation, and many faces and names came to mind as I pressed in to considering the many joys flowing from this doctrine. One particular delight that kept surfacing as I worked through the material was related to the notion of repentance. Now, I know, it may not seem obvious how the doctrine of preservation should color our understanding of repentance, but there is much joy to be had in bringing these two Christian ideas together.

The thought that continues to stir joy in my soul is rather simple: God's preservation of his people reminds us that *even our stumbling* happens within the covenantal grip of grace. We know that when we fall, when we stumble, and when we sin, that does *nothing* to our preservation. Our preservation is not solid because of our ability not to sin. Now, this is not to downplay the significance of our striving for holiness and mortifying sin. However, we are not preserved *because* of our ability to put off sin; rather we put off sin *because* God has redeemed us and preserves us.

This means when we do fall, when we do sin, there is no need to think that we must start from the beginning. Rather, we realize the very sin we have committed has already been crucified and atoned for, and with that gospel realization we begin to mortify and continue on our pilgrimage toward Christ. There is a restfulness even in our repentance, knowing our Father knows we will fail. He has paid for our failing in the death of his Son, and in the covenantal grip of the Triune God, we get back up and continue the process of being conformed into the perfect image of Christ.

This means we do not have to make the mistake of Eden. When Adam and Eve sinned, their impulse—due to guilt and shame—was to run *away* from God and hide from him (Gen. 3:8). Rather, because we know God will preserve his people because of his goodness, when we sin, we can run *to* God as the only One who can actually do something with our sin. So, then, may we join the chorus of Jude's benediction: "To *him* who is able to *keep you from stumbling* and *to present you blameless* before the presence of his glory with great joy, to the only God, our Savior, through Jesus Christ our Lord, be glory, majesty, dominion, and authority, before all time and now and forever. Amen" (Jude 24–25).

9

Ecclesiology

Delighting in Your Community

The church is not merely a place we attend but a people to whom we belong. The local church should be a place where we hear the question of Cain and Abel—"Am I my brother's keeper?"—and answer with an emphatic *yes* (Gen. 4:9). The church is a body of people with whom we march arm in arm toward the promised land, seeing to it that no one fails to cross the Jordan but that each of us keeps our eyes on Jesus until our faith is turned to sight.

Introducing the Doctrine of Ecclesiology

I am in agreement with that great nineteenth-century prince of preachers, Charles Spurgeon, who once famously said that the church should be the dearest place on earth to us believers. Contrary to the pervasive view of the church in our age, Spurgeon writes:

> Give yourself to the Church. You that are members of the Church have not found it perfect and I hope that you feel almost

> glad that you have not. If I had never joined a Church till I had found one that was perfect, I would never have joined one at all! And the moment I did join it, if I had found one, I should have spoiled it, for it would not have been a perfect Church after I had become a member of it. Still, imperfect as it is, *it is the dearest place on earth to us.*[1]

What Spurgeon called "the dearest place on earth" is often forgotten, ignored, or even disliked by so many evangelical Christians today. For many Christians today, the church is an unfortunate addition to an otherwise fine-enough faith. A pervasive attitude suggests that it is more than acceptable—even preferable—to take Jesus and leave the church. As if it is permissible to love the Groom but despise his bride.

What makes the modern distaste for the local church worse, I am afraid, is that many people are despising or denouncing something they do not truly know. I give an assignment to students each semester, without warning, on the first day of our ecclesiology unit. I have students answer the question, "What is a church?" in less than a hundred words. Because I am not an evil professor, I do not grade the assignment, but every semester, it is obvious that students have the ability to point to a church—"There is one right there"—but are not equipped to succinctly, biblically, and theologically define exactly what a church *is*. This assignment is helpful in showing them that today there are far more opinions about what the church ought to *do* than there is wisdom about what a church actually *is*. In our day, the heat is high on opinions about God's people, but the light is low; there is more passion than wisdom.

To be sure, the church is far from perfect. There are many who have a bad taste in their mouths regarding the church due

1. Charles H. Spurgeon, "The Best Donation," in *The Metropolitan Tabernacle Pulpit*, vol. 37, 1891.

to no fault of their own. They have felt firsthand the deep pain caused by hypocritical Christians, whether through an unbiblically unwelcoming environment, pastors bringing shame to the name of Christ through moral failings, leaders being more interested in receiving applause than seeking the good of their neighbors, or abuse that seems rampant in so many corners of the church today. To call the church "the dearest place on earth" is not to downplay any of these. In fact, a biblical view of what the church ought to be makes its pains and failures more severe, for the place that should have been rich soil where souls can thrive was the location of horrendous actions.

Some people believe the church is sinless and incapable of wrongdoing, while others view it as the root of all our problems and incapable of doing any good. I wish to put away these caricatures and say that, as ugly and disappointing as she can be, God has called us to love his bride.

The church will likely never move from being a mere place we attend to a people we belong to if we do not give ourselves to considering what God intends for this people—us people—to be. The beauty and glory that are God's church will stay hidden from our mind's eye if we do not open our Scriptures and see just how wonderous his design of the church is. It is easy to say, "We ought to love the church," but my hope is that understanding some of the theology behind God's design for local churches will help move some readers from a place of begrudgingly attending a local body to seeing their local assembly as grace upon grace—a covenant people, committed to making sure we all receive the inheritance of our faith and see Jesus face-to-face.

It is impossible to do justice to all the wonder and beauty in the field of ecclesiology—the study of the church—in a single chapter, especially one of this length. However, I would like to consider a few doctrines and practices within the field of ecclesiology in hopes of framing the church as a covenant people ordained by God and given as a gift to his children. To move toward this goal, we'll discuss the definition of a church along with a covenantal understanding of membership and discipline within the church.

Defining the Doctrine of Ecclesiology

In the chapter on Scripture, I discussed how knowing *what* type of literature we are reading impacts *how* we read the literature. For example, we read a newspaper advertisement much differently than we read a novel. Likewise, when it comes to studying the doctrine of the church, knowing *what* the church is will have significant implications for our convictions about what the church ought to *do*. The theological way to say this truth is: Ecclesial ontology should precede ecclesial function. The key to thinking well about the activity of the church is sustained attention on the definition and purpose of the church.

This is something I must remind students of often, especially undergraduate students, who often have strong convictions about what the church ought to *do*. My classroom is full of passionate people who desperately want to love their neighbors well, and they have fire in their bones about a million good works the church may set her sights on. I like to remind them, however, that there is often much heat about what the church ought to do without much light about what the church is. I like to encourage them with this advice: Before you approach your pastors with a list of complaints about all the church is not doing and all the things they should be doing, be sure you can first actually give a definition of what the church is according to God's Word.

There have been numerous definitions of what exactly a church is throughout its history. The Reformers argued that anywhere there was right preaching of the Word and the right administration of the sacraments, there you had a true church.[2] Dutch theologian Herman Bavinck, who has had a profound influence on me, once said, "The community of those who share in Christ and his benefits is called 'the church.'"[3] While these definitions are quite helpful and should craft our imagination as to what a church is to be and do, I particularly like the definition recently put forward by Jonathan Leeman in his book *Church Membership*: "A local church is a group of Christians who regularly gather in Christ's name to officially affirm and oversee one another's membership in Jesus Christ and his kingdom through gospel preaching and gospel ordinances."[4] This definition emphasizes five major points. Each makes the definition worthwhile and advantageous, and while each point deserves a more robust elaboration, allow me to just state each one in brief, in hopes that doing so will help us round out what "church" means.

First, Leeman begins by asserting that a local church is a "group of *Christians*." As we will see below in our section on church membership and discipline, this is a significant emphasis that will cause severe damage if not heeded. Of course, Leeman and I both write from a Baptistic framework for local church governance and authority, but even those who do not share our Baptist convictions ought to have a high view of church membership and church discipline.

Second, Leeman notes that a local church ought to "regularly gather." Hebrews 10:25 instructs us not to forsake the gathering of the saints. We are an embodied people who, by virtue of the role we are to play in one another's lives, must meet together.

2. John Calvin, "Prefatory Address by John Calvin to Francis I, King of France (1536)," in *Institutes of the Christian Religion*, trans. Henry Beveridge (Hendrickson, 2008), xxix.

3. Herman Bavinck, *Reformed Dogmatics*, vol. 4, ed. John Bolt (Baker Academic, 2004), 275.

4. Jonathan Leeman, *Church Membership: How the World Knows Who Represents Jesus* (Crossway, 2010), 63.

Even the root of the word *ekklesia* gets at the notion of that gathering. In a world that seems to get ever more digital, ever more isolated, and ever lonelier, we are those who know the beauty in seeing each other face-to-face in real time and space. We insist on actual gathering, that we can truly know and love one another as we journey toward Christ together.

Third, Leeman rightly notes that a local church is to "officially affirm and oversee one another's membership in Jesus Christ and his kingdom." We are not those with a mere loose connection who happen to wander into the same building every Sunday. Rather, we play a remarkably important role in one another's lives—an authoritative role of support and care. We are to affirm one another and give biblical oversight to one another's membership in the gospel.

Fourth, something easy to miss in Leeman's definition is that we gather "in Christ's name." The local church ought to be an outpost for the kingdom of God. We are the body of Christ, and the body ought to act in line with the head. The church ought to represent Christ, as we are ambassadors for Christ.

Fifth and finally, God has not only called us to be a people who affirm and oversee one another's membership in Christ and his kingdom but also given us the tools by which we practice this affirmation and oversight: "gospel preaching and gospel ordinances." The ordinances are covenantal signs: Baptism is the entry sign that someone has entered the covenant, and the Lord's Supper is the reoccurring nurturing and sustaining sign of membership in the new covenant people. It is through these covenantal signs that we can affirm (through administering baptism) or deny (through withholding the Lord's Supper) one another in the new covenant community.

Church Membership and Church Discipline

In a covenantal view of ecclesiology—where the church is not merely a place to attend but a people to whom to belong—a significant concern is that those who make up the church are regenerate Christians who have the Holy Spirit. If we are going to walk through our days with these brothers and sisters in a way in which they have authority over our lives and, as our definition says, are going to "affirm and oversee" our "membership in Jesus Christ and his kingdom," we need to be confident that those who have such authority are Christians whom we can trust with this severe privilege and responsibility.

This means we ought to have a high view of both church membership and church discipline. Not only do those in our churches have a privileged position of authority over our lives, but we are also to "gather in Christ's name." Local churches ought to be local manifestations of the kingdom where we represent Christ, gather in his name, and, by the way we love one another and our neighbor, demonstrate what a kingdom ethic and life in Christ ought to look like. Therefore, when we affirm someone into membership in our churches, we are not only giving them authority over us but also affirming that they, by virtue of the gospel they confess and the way they live their lives as gospel confessors, are representative of the kingdom. This only drives home the reality of how vital it is that those who make up our churches are regenerate believers.

Church Membership

When it comes to church membership, there is a vital question that deserves a moment's attention. That question is simply, "Is church membership biblical?" I get this question often from well-meaning students, and it makes sense as there is no chapter and verse we can point to that explicitly commands church membership. Scripture doesn't come right out and say, "You must join a local congregation, and this means more than mere attendance." However, as has often been said by others and as I often say to my own students: I think we can say that while church membership is *nowhere* explicitly mentioned or commanded in the Scriptures, it is *everywhere* assumed.

Seeing this vital point regarding church membership's biblical status takes both biblical reading and biblical reasoning. Consider just a few lines of reason from the Scriptures that seem to point toward a form of membership in a local congregation. First, in Matthew, Christ states that entering the kingdom of God means being bound to the church "on earth," and it is in local contexts that we see the church on earth (Matt. 16:16–19; 18:17–19).

Second, Hebrews 13:17 calls Christians to "obey your leaders and submit to them." A natural question here is, "Which leaders?" Are we supposed to submit to all leaders, all pastors, all elders everywhere? Of course not. The command suggests that one can know *which* leaders one must submit to and obey. There seems to be some way we know which elders give oversight to our souls.

Third, the verse continues, "Obey your leaders and submit to them, for they are keeping watch over your souls, as those who will have to give an account" (Heb. 13:17). The question about this clause, similar to the second, is, "Who are these elders expected to give an account *for*?" As with the second question, it cannot be all Christians everywhere. Rather, there seems to be an identifiable group of Christians for which these elders will give an account for how they handled their souls.

Fourth, Paul seems to give explicit reference to some being "inside the church" and others being "outside" the church (1 Cor. 5:12–13). This seems to be not a casual association but rather an identifiable way of determining who is numbered among the church and who is not.

Fifth, and similarly, the church in Corinth seems to consist of a definite number of Christians, as Paul is able to speak of "punishment by the majority" in reference to church discipline (2 Cor. 2:6). There seems to be some formal way of identifying the whole of the church, such that the majority of the church can inflict the punishment of church discipline.

Sixth, there seems to be a network of letter writing on behalf of believers in the New Testament. We can see this in a number of places in Scripture (Acts 18:27; 2 Cor. 3:1; Col. 4:10). Again, though not an explicit argument, this does suggest the local church was careful to vet the genuineness of faith of those on the outside of their usual gathering. These missives acted as letters of recommendation to attest that the faith and fidelity of individual Christians were legitimate for other bodies of believers.

Seventh and finally, there seems to be something of an argument for church membership in the multitude of "one another" passages in Scripture. We are called to "encourage" one another (1 Thess. 5:11), to have a posture of "bearing with one another in love" (Eph. 4:2), to "be kind to one another" (v. 32), to "bear one another's burdens" (Gal. 6:2), to "exhort one another" (Heb. 3:13), to "consider how to stir up one another to love and good works" (10:24), to "not [neglect] to meet together" (v. 25), to "count others more significant than yourselves" (Phil. 2:3), to "confess [our] sins to one another" (James 5:16), to "live in harmony" with one another (Rom. 12:16), and to "use [our gifts] to serve one another" (1 Pet. 4:10). These passages are but a handful of the "one another" passages scattered throughout the whole of the New Testament.

Of course, as someone trying to follow Christ, I should have these postures as much as I am able for all Christians everywhere. However, the reality is that if I am called to "bear the burdens," for example, of all Christians *everywhere*, I may find that I bear the burdens of no Christians *anywhere*. Rather, if I am called to bear the burdens of *these* Christians, my love moves from the *idea* of my neighbor to my *actual* neighbor in front of me—a point we will pick up again later.

These arguments are not the totality for what a biblical defense of the doctrine of church membership looks like from the New Testament, but they are enough to demonstrate that the practice of church membership may not be explicitly stated but perhaps is assumed. Having an identifiable way to assess who I am responsible for and who is responsible for me seems to be so foundational to the New Testament church that it undergirds the rest of the commands of Scripture.

Church membership is a doctrine in which the covenantal structure of the church meets the belonging our souls so desperately need. Part of the good news of the gospel is that when God redeems our souls, it is not redemption toward an isolated life. On the contrary, we are redeemed into the fellowship *of the redeemed* and get the high privilege of journeying through the Christian life with God's people.

Church Discipline

The covenantal shape of belonging entails the notion of covenantal accountability. If membership is the covenantal acceptance into the community of saints, then discipline is the covenantal maintenance of the community's holiness. In this light, church discipline is far from a harsh intrusion or a betrayal but the loving outworking of faithfulness to Christ whereby the church seeks to correct the wandering, protect the flock, and purify the church's witness among the nations.

Often, theologians describe church discipline in two lanes. First, there is formative discipline: the ongoing rhythm of teaching, exhortation, and correction that shapes believers into Christlikeness. We are all being *discipled* into Christ's image, and this form of discipline ought to shape everyone in the church. Second, there is corrective discipline, which is what our minds more often think of regarding "church discipline." Corrective discipline involves the sober process of confronting sin in a member of the body of Christ through a process both individual and, if needed, corporate, with the hope of repentance and restoration.

Unlike the doctrine of church membership, the doctrine of church discipline is not merely implicitly assumed in the biblical text but explicitly commanded. This means that church discipline is not optional but essential for ecclesial fidelity to the Lord. Jesus himself entrusted the keys of the kingdom to the church (Matt. 16:19; 18:18), authorizing the church to bind and loose, to affirm and warn. Paul commands the Corinthians to remove the unrepentant sinner from fellowship, not as an act of condemnation but as an act of love that both awakens the sinner and preserves the church's witness (1 Cor. 5:1–7). Discipline, then, is not contrary to grace but an expression of it—a sign that God loves his people enough to guard their holiness.

When it comes to church discipline, a number of passages have importance for the conversation, but three come to the forefront: Matthew 18:15–18; 1 Corinthians 5:1–7; and 2 Corinthians 2:6–11. From these passages, I would like to draw out five important items to notice.

First, church discipline has a defined process. As seen in the Matthew passage, Christ gives the church a reasonable approach to church discipline that starts with individual accountability and leads to corporate accountability.

Second, church discipline is *always* for the sake of restoration. As we see in the 1 Corinthians passage, discipline is "so that his spirit may be saved in the day of the Lord" (5:5). This means church discipline will never be done in a faithful manner if it is done with vengeance or ill will. Church discipline ought to be done with a lump in our throat and tears in our eyes as we are desperate for our brothers and sisters to return to fidelity.

Third, we discipline for the sake of the purity of the whole church. Again in 1 Corinthians, Paul tells us, "Do you not know that a little leaven leavens the whole lump?" (5:6). Since we are one body, as the church, if one of the members of our body is sick, the whole of the body will be sick. In this way, church discipline resembles Old Testament practices, such as when a tribe was called to put a member sick with an infection outside the camp so that the rest of the camp would not get infected (Lev. 13:45–46). When the infection was healed, the brother or sister who had been sick could come back into the camp.

Fourth, church discipline is to be done as "the church." Paul writes, "When you are assembled in the name of the Lord Jesus . . . deliver this man to Satan" (1 Cor. 5:4–5). In the 2 Corinthians passage, Paul calls discipline the "punishment by the majority" (2:6). This seems to suggest that it is in the context of the gathered assembly that the church has the right and responsibility of utilizing the keys of the kingdom.

Fifth, based on all the above, church discipline ought to benefit (1) the person being disciplined, as they see the seriousness of their unrepentance, (2) the church that is doing the discipline, as they become a healthier and more whole body, and (3) the watching world, as the church corporately says not to watch or believe the gospel of *this* person, since there is corporate doubt about their salvation.

Ecclesiology's Lasting Beauty

To bring this section to a close, I will simply say that, as broken as the church can be, this bride has changed my life. She was there when my mother passed away and when my wife and I suffered the pain of infertility and multiple miscarriages. She is there today when my inner voice sounds like the adversary and not the advocate, when I mourn and when I rejoice, and as I stumble my way toward the promised land—keeping watch over my soul and walking with me and my family.

Unlike other chapters, this one is titled after an entire location of theology. Ecclesiology is more than just one doctrine; it is an entire field of theology in which there are many doctrines worthy of exploration. In this chapter, we have not even begun to discuss the wonderful doctrines of the sacraments of baptism and the Lord's Supper; the significance of polity (church structure) and the various shapes of church governance; the offices of the church and the remarkable way the Lord uses pastors, elders, and deacons in the life of Christians; the rhythms and liturgies of the church during gathered worship; and so much more. Ecclesiology contains treasure after treasure. Give yourself to sustained consideration of God's design for the church, and you will find enough impetus for worship for the rest of your days.

Delighting in the Doctrine of Ecclesiology

For many Christians, ecclesiology in general and the church in particular can be treated as an unfortunate add-on in the Christian faith. Many want Jesus but find his bride—and the people who make it up—to be something they begrudgingly accept. It ought not be so. Scripture seems to speak of the church among the preeminent blessings of being united to Christ and presents the church not as some institution bearing little significance but as a people among whom God has chosen to dwell. The doctrine of the church presses against our instincts toward isolation and self-sufficiency; a biblical understanding of the church shows that the Christian life is fundamentally a shared life. To delight in ecclesiology, then, is to discover that God has woven our communion with him together with our communion with one another. God's people are not an optional add-on in our pilgrimage of following Christ. The church is not an obstacle to spiritual vitality but one of its chief means. We should, then, press in to just a few of the myriad beauties and delights of the many doctrines that make up ecclesiology.

Covenantal Belonging in a World of Isolation

In 1982, a well-known British pastor named John Stott published a book called *I Believe in Preaching*. In the book, Stott considers how the church may handle technological advancement in the future. He writes about the roles of face-to-face interaction, the local church gathering, and preaching as technology continues to develop. Of course, Stott was asking these questions before the advent of the smartphone, social media, or the dawn of artificial intelligence.

Scott, trying to envision the future, predicted this about the growing use of technology:

> It is difficult to imagine the world in the year A.D. 2000, by which time versatile micro-processors are likely to be as common as simple calculators are today. We should certainly welcome the fact that the silicon chip will transcend human brainpower, as the machine has transcended human muscle-power. Much less welcome will be the probable reduction of human contact, as the new electronic network renders personal relationships ever less necessary.

Stott continues, more accurately than he could have known:

> In such a dehumanized society the fellowship of the local church will become increasingly important, whose members meet one another and talk and listen to one another in person rather than on screen. In this human context of mutual love, the speaking and hearing of the Word of God is also likely to become more necessary for the preservation of our humanness, not less.[5]

We cannot know, of course, but I wonder if Stott's wildest imagination could have predicted just how correct he was. Could he have envisioned the kind of loneliness epidemic we

5. John Stott, *I Believe in Preaching*, 2nd ed. (Hodder Publishing, 1998), 69.

face in our world today? We are a people with more faces in front of us than probably any time before, yet they are mediated by screens and filters. We are a people who can micropublish and broadcast nearly every facet of our lives, yet we are rarely truly *known*.

This is the product not only of developing technology but also of modern Western culture's idolization of choice, independence, and expressive individualism. Against these headwinds, covenantal membership in a local church stands as a countertestimony. Ecclesiology, then, is not merely abstract theory about the idea of a perfect church but a lived covenantal reality. In the ordinary rhythms of congregational life—hearing the Word preached, sharing the Lord's Supper, exercising church membership and discipline, overseeing one another as confessors, and making our confessions—the covenant of God takes visible, communal form. To belong to a church is to embody the beautiful truth that God has not designed the pilgrimage that is the Christian life to be a sojourn of loneliness. Rather, it is *together* that we assemble each Lord's day, it is *together* that we weep with those who weep and rejoice with those who rejoice, it is *together* that we exercise the keys of the kingdom, and it is—one day—*together* that we will arrive on that golden shore.

Love Your Neighbor, Not the Idea of Your Neighbor

My favorite novel of all time is *The Brothers Karamazov* by Russian literary master Fyodor Dostoevsky. How ever many words I have spilled to get this far in the book you hold, I could likely spend the same amount (or more) detailing the many, many reasons the story of the Karamazov brothers moves me. Among my favorite scenes in the book is a conversation between two of the brothers—Alyosha and Ivan. These brothers share the same DNA but differ substantially in their worldview. Alyosha, four years younger than Ivan, is a monk and devoted to the religious life. His brother, however, wavers somewhere between atheism and religious doubt.

While the two brothers dialogue frequently in the novel, this particular conversation takes place in a café and is occasioned by Ivan Karamazov's eventual departure for Moscow. The brothers, whom Dostoevsky uses throughout the novel to represent differing philosophical, psychological, and theological poles, are lamenting the fact that they do not truly *know each other*. They have spent much time around each other, yes, but they fear they have little depth in their relationship. Their desire to press in to greater relational depth and brotherly fraternity causes them to move into weighty subjects, including the relationship between love and religion.

During this fictional conversation, Ivan makes a great confession that real-life folks like you and I may not admit as readily but, nevertheless, can often functionally embody. In short, he confesses to his younger brother Alyosha that he completely understands loving the *idea* of people in general but that he has never really loved *actual* people. "I never could understand how it's possible to love one's neighbors. In my opinion, it is precisely one's neighbors that one cannot possibly love. Perhaps if they weren't so nigh," he says, and later adds, "It's still possible to love one's neighbor abstractly, and even occasionally from a distance, but hardly ever up close."[6] This is a startling difference from a previous line by another character, one who embodies sacrificial love and truth, who says, "Love in action is a harsh and dreadful thing compared with love in dreams."[7]

6. Fyodor Dostoevsky, *The Brothers Karamazov* (Knopf, 1992), 236–37.

7. Dostoevsky, *Brothers Karamazov*, 58. Some of this section is taken from an article I wrote for Midwestern Seminary's The Lord and Literature series. See Ronni Kurtz, "Love People, Not the Idea of People: A Lesson from Ivan Karamazov," For the Church, May 18, 2021, https://ftc.co/resource-library/blog-entries/love-people-not-the-idea-of-people-a-lesson-from-ivan-karamazov/. Used by permission.

What does this conversation between Ivan and Alyosha Karamazov have to do with ecclesiology? In this scene, what Ivan is bemoaning is the inconvenience of the particularities and the nearness of his neighbors. It is easy to love others, to love people, to love humankind, to even love your neighbor, if your neighbor does not have a name and does not have particular needs that beg to be met. If you can keep your neighbor at a safe distance and are not confronted with any of the valleys of their life, they are quite an easy person to love. However, this all changes when your neighbor becomes *near*. When your neighbor sees your face every Sunday, attends your Bible study regularly, and frequents your home for small group meetings, their unique characteristics and needs are obvious. These needs often ask you, *will* you love not just "your neighbor" but *this* neighbor?

To make the point clear: In a covenantal understanding of church membership, it should be near impossible to love merely the idea of our neighbor. Church membership is not satisfied with you and me loving the idea of people; it calls us to love and care for *these* people.

At my church, we partake in the Lord's Supper every Sunday. As the church lines up to receive the elements, I often try to remind my soul, *these ones—it is* these ones *you must know and love*. The lineup for the Lord's Supper is a parade of saints, covenant church members who have all experienced the miracle of regeneration, and when they are in front of my eyes every Lord's day, my neighbor is remarkably near, remarkably particular. Church membership will not allow me to neglect their messy particularities, as if "love in dreams" is an adequate substitute for "love in action."

And in case it is not obvious: Your particularities, with all your messiness and mess-ups in view, you in all your *you-ness*, are also *their* concern in church membership. You and your near neighbors, in church membership, are each other's problem as you march arm in arm toward the promised land in covenantal relationship.

A Voice Louder Than Your Own

Maybe not as obvious a point as the first two in this section but one that has been personally significant in my own life is this: When one is prone to listen to a broken inner voice, the collective voice of the church can speak a louder and better word. As I have mentioned, I struggle with a strong inner self-critical voice. My sinful tendency toward an antigospel inner voice can often usher before my conscience a rather strong case for why I am still under condemnation and why guilt and shame still hang around my neck.

This is where it can be advantageous to be an actual member of a biblically healthy church rather than a mere attender of a church. Due to the covenant framework of membership in my local church, my fellow church members know me. Not everyone in the church knows me deeply, but a handful of members know my struggles—they know what stirs my affection for Jesus, and they know when my communion with Christ is cold. They know me well enough to recognize the warning signs that I am beginning to listen to who my insecurities tell me I am rather than who I have been declared to be in Christ. Not only can I listen to these brothers and sisters speak truth into my life when I am tempted to believe lies, but, along with them, I can also listen to the voice of the *entire* church body.

Since the local church is the primary vehicle in which God has designed the overseeing of our souls—especially seen in church membership and discipline—every Sunday, when my church allows me to come to the Lord's Table and participate in communion, they are, with one corporate voice, saying that *they* believe the gospel is real in my life. With one corporate voice, and without saying a word, they speak assurance into my soul. So I have a choice to make when my insecurity flares up: I can listen to my broken inner voice of insecurity, or I can listen to the voice of this gathered assembly, both her pastors and her members, as they allow me access to the table and continued membership. This point may not seem important for some readers, but for those of us who have an overactive inner critic, there can be profound delight in the corporate voice of God's people speaking assurance to our souls.

10

Eschatology

Delighting in the End

My daughter is about to turn five years old, and this Easter season has proved to be the source of a flood of questions. It is the first year the notion that Jesus *died* is hitting her in ways both profound and quite scary. She is thinking about death for the first time, and therefore thinking about resurrection for the first time too.

One morning, as she is helping me cook breakfast, I can tell she is disturbed. After some prodding, she asks a question that shatters my heart as a father. She asks, "Dada, when I die, will you make sure that Nutmeg is by my body so that when I rise again, I will be able to see her right away?" Nutmeg is my daughter's beloved stuffed bunny rabbit, which she takes *everywhere* and has been a constant companion since she was just a few days old.

The question causes a few moments of chaos in my head as I fumble for the right answer. The first thing I feel is deep sorrow that death is not merely an abstraction; her question has a correct premise because one day she will die. I, of course, know this in theory, but hearing it in her small voice shatters me. It grips my heart and, in some ways, brings the sorrow of the day to come when she breathes her last breath into the kitchen that morning in a way I had not felt before. The thought makes my hatred for sin vitriolic. I hate that she will die. I hate that sin will cause her pain. Yet, while her question brings sorrow, it also brings a profound thankfulness that for all my fatherly hatred of sin and death, I can hold out hope that these two terrors will not have the final word in my daughter's life. Even in her question is the *correct* assumption that she will rise again.

Introducing the Doctrine of Eschatology

As I write these words, that interaction is about a week behind me, and now that both the sorrow of considering her death and the joy of considering her resurrection have settled a bit, a new emotion has come to me—one of *wonder*. As my daughter processed the good news of rising again in the resurrection, the *best* thing her four-year-old brain could conceive of was the notion that she would get to be reunited with her stuffed animal. For a few days following our talk, I began to think about how it is my job to disciple her thoughts over the next few decades of her life to see just how much more glory and beauty is coming for those who are united to Christ in the resurrection. While it will take time, I want her to see that her thoughts of the life to come are *too small*; while getting Nutmeg again may be great to her mind now, she has no conception of the magnificent beauty awaiting her.

As I was thinking about the duty of a dad to disciple his daughter's theological imagination, another thought struck me: I am confident that I also have a view of the resurrection and the life to come that is far too small, far too lacking in beauty. I am sure, with all my years of study, all my contemplation, and a doctoral degree in theology, that when I conceive of what life across the Jordan will look like, it is the conceptual equivalent to being reunited with a stuffed bunny rabbit.

Eschatology contains beauty unimaginable. Therefore, turning our mind's eye toward "the end" ought to discipline our souls to contemplate and consider the beauty to come, even if our wildest and deepest thoughts only scratch the surface of the true profundity of eternity. That is my goal in this chapter. My hope here is to examine, even if briefly, three glorious doctrines of the Christian faith—the resurrection, glorification, and the beatific vision—in hopes of seeing and feeling the beauty of what is awaiting the end of each Christian's earthly pilgrimage. These three doctrines will not cover all that is considered eschatology but will grow our ability to see the beauty of a Christian understanding of the end.

Defining the Doctrine of Eschatology

The field of eschatology concerns itself with the end, or "the last things." Questions and opinions about *how* the world is going to end, *when* the world is going to end, *what will happen* when the world ends, and others like these are so prevalent in our day, and were so prevalent in the last few centuries, that it can be hard to even start making heads or tails of where to begin thinking about eschatology. Given the sheer amount of literature written and the vast difference of opinions on eschatology, it can be easy to make one of two mistakes in this field of theology: obsession or neglect.

These two errors can become ditches on either side of a faithful eschatological road that we should seek to avoid. Some theologians have referred to them as *eschatomania* and *eschatophobia*. Eschatomania, or a propensity to make *too much* of eschatology, is a kind of eschatological obsession. These individuals may turn every headline into a prophecy and every political event into a coded signal of the end times. For them, eschatology becomes a system of speculation rather than a source of hope. There is a temptation to get wrapped up in trying to chart events in Scripture and history and get so pulled into questions of chronology that we forget the primary purpose and telos of eschatological thinking: to keep our eyes on Christ, our ultimate reward and goal.

On the other side of the road is a contrasting error of making *too little* of eschatology—eschatophobia—which is often a pendulum swing to eschatology done poorly. These people argue that there is little we can know about the end, and we should not focus on last things because they have little to do with our current, everyday lives. These Christians erroneously see the return of Christ as a vague theological concept rather than the longed-for day that ought to shape our present lives. The fact that the King of the cosmos is coming back to judge the living and the dead has little to do with how they imagine the world.

This is not how the Scriptures describe eschatology. In the New Testament, for example, it is quite obvious that Jesus and Paul have eschatology as a strong working category in their thoughts, affections, and ethics. Paul, for example, can say, "I consider that the sufferings of this present time are not worth comparing with the glory that is to be revealed to us" (Rom. 8:18), showing that eschatology forms his theology of suffering. Elsewhere, he writes, "Our citizenship is in heaven, and from it we await a Savior, the Lord Jesus Christ, who will transform our lowly body to be like his glorious body" (Phil. 3:20–21). These two passages are but a small sample of how eschatology shapes Paul's imagination and, in turn, his life and ministry.

The reality of the Christian life is that we are all on a pilgrimage back *to* the Triune God, since all things are from, through, and to him. One day we will indeed see our Lord come back to judge the living and the dead, and one day we will indeed cross the Jordan. Healthy eschatology, then, lives between the two extremes. It does not demand charts and timelines, but it does demand hope. Biblical eschatology reorients us toward eternity, not through mere escapism but by anchoring our day-to-day toil with faithfulness in the sure promise of Christ's return and the fulfillment of all he has spoken. With this in mind—in hopes to avoid unhealthy eschatomania and eschatophobia—we now can turn our attention to three doctrines in the field of eschatology: the resurrection, glorification, and the beatific vision.

The Resurrection

Since Jesus is the head of the church and we are all grafted into him as the life-giving vine, we will go where he goes.

Christ's Resurrection

Our Lord Jesus Christ has been resurrected, and we will be too. As the head goes, so goes the body, as Paul tells the church in Rome: "For if we have been united with him in a death like his, we shall certainly be united with him in a resurrection like his" (Rom. 6:5). And to the church in Thessalonica, he writes, "For since we believe that Jesus died and rose again, even so, through Jesus, God will bring with him those who have fallen asleep" (1 Thess. 4:14). So, the starting place for our own resurrection is the resurrection of our Lord, Jesus Christ.

We are flirting with the impossible if we hope to put into words just how significant that moment is when Jesus Christ of Nazareth rises from the grave. Indeed, we could argue that this very moment—when he pushes open the tomb and walks out—is the single most important moment in our cosmos. Paul finds this moment so significant that he writes, "If Christ has not been raised, your faith is futile and you are still in your sins," and he continues, "If in Christ we have hope in this life only, we are of all people most to be pitied" (1 Cor. 15:17, 19). If we strip the resurrection from Christianity, we are left with a devastated hollowness—a cross without victory, a gospel without good news, a Savior still dead. If Christ is not risen, then Paul's question—"O death, where is your victory?"—has a countermeaning that would be the end of our faith (v. 55).

But this is not the Christian story. The Christian story is one in which a carpenter from Nazareth puts death to death. The second person of the Trinity—the eternal Son of God—becomes the temporal son of Mary, and through his perfect life, subversion of death, and victorious resurrection he fulfills all the prophets had long foretold and grants life to the wayward. When talking about our Christ, we have the question of the angels on our lips as it pertains to his resurrection: "Why do you seek the living among the dead? He is not here, but has risen" (Luke 24:5–6).

The dead body of Christ that lay in the tomb began to breathe again, blood began to pump through his veins, his eyes opened, and on that great day when he rose again, death was put to death. What started with the resurrection of Jesus Christ of Nazareth will eventually culminate in our own resurrection. One day that seed that is our death—like a flower in cosmic bloom—will push up from the ground and erupt into a glorious resurrection.

Our Resurrection

As it relates to theological and biblical specifics concerning our resurrection, there are a few things the biblical data seems to allow us to say. While I will not spend substantial time here, a few particulars about the doctrine of our resurrection are worth noting.

First, I am convinced that when Christians die, they will not need to wait to be with our Lord. Our souls will immediately be with him while our physical bodies await the final resurrection. This is not a new idea but rather is consistent in the church's history. Question 37 of the Westminster Shorter Catechism asks, "What benefits do believers receive from Christ at death?" Countless Christians over the last several hundred years have memorized the answer: "The souls of believers are, at their death, made perfect in holiness, and do immediately pass into glory: and their bodies, being still united to Christ, do rest in their graves until the resurrection."[1]

This should not be a surprise to us, as our Lord himself said to the thief on the cross in the last hours of his life, "Truly, I say to you, *today* you will be with me in paradise" (Luke 23:43). Another significant passage to consider here is Paul's words to the church in Corinth: "So we are always of good courage. We know that while we are at home in the body *we are away from the Lord*, for we walk by faith, not by sight. Yes, we are of good courage, and we would rather *be away from the body and at home with the Lord*" (2 Cor. 5:6–8). While it may not be the primary exegetical point of the passage, it seems that Paul's words would at least have us know that it is possible to be *away from the body*, and to be so is to be with the Lord.

Writing on what happens to Christians at the moment of death, Herman Bavinck gives a helpful answer when he asks and answers an important question:

> When do believers cease to be pilgrims and arrive in their homeland? To this question Scripture has but one answer: at death. Nowhere does it represent the godly after death as still being tormented by punishment or suffering due to sin. The godly always express as their certain expectation that at death they will have reached the end of their pilgrimage and entrance into the eternal blessed life in heaven (Ps. 73:24–25; Luke 23:43; Acts 7:59; 2 Cor. 5:1; Phil. 1:23; 2 Tim. 4:7).[2]

1. "The Westminster Shorter Catechism: Q37," The Westminster Standard, accessed January 12, 2026, https://thewestminsterstandard.org/westminster-shorter-catechism/.

2. Bavinck, *Reformed Dogmatics*, vol. 4, ed. John Bolt (Baker Academic, 2004), 635–36.

Second, while our souls will indeed immediately be with the Lord, it is vital we confess a literal bodily resurrection. From the Old Testament through the culmination of the New Testament, the literal resurrection of the dead is a consistent theme. Jesus himself says, "And as for the resurrection of the dead, have you not read what was said to you by God: 'I am the God of Abraham, and the God of Isaac, and the God of Jacob'? He is not God of the dead, but of the living" (Matt. 22:31–32). This Jesus, the eternally generated One who assumed flesh, by virtue of his aseity and power over life itself, will call us out of the grave. Jesus reminds us that this power belongs to him when he says, "Truly, truly, I say to you, an hour is coming, and is now here, when the dead will hear the voice of the Son of God, and those who hear will live. For as the Father has life in himself, so he has granted the Son also to have life in himself" (John 5:25–26). Jesus continues, "Do not marvel at this, for an hour is coming when all who are in the tombs will hear his voice and come out, those who have done good to the resurrection of life, and those who have done evil to the resurrection of judgment" (vv. 28–29).

As we have already seen, the resurrection of Christ is a foretaste of our resurrection, and we know his resurrection is a literal, bodily resurrection, for Thomas was able to touch the wounds on Christ's very person (20:24–27). It may be the resurrection of the body is nowhere in Scripture addressed more directly than when Paul describes a hypothetical person questioning, "How are the dead raised? With what kind of body do they come?" (1 Cor. 15:35). He continues to explain what some theologians have called the continuity and discontinuity of the resurrected body: There is continuity in that it will be *our* body, but there is discontinuity in that it will be our *glorified* body. So, contrasting the nonglorified body and the glorified heavenly body, Paul writes:

> So it is with the resurrection of the dead. What is sown is perishable; what is raised is imperishable. It is sown in dishonor; it is raised in glory. It is sown in weakness; it is raised in power. It is sown a natural body; it is raised a spiritual body. If there is a natural body, there is also a spiritual body. . . . Behold! I tell you a mystery. We shall not all sleep, but we shall all be changed, in a moment, in the twinkling of an eye, at the last trumpet. For the trumpet will sound, and the dead will be raised imperishable, and we shall be changed. For this perishable body must put on the imperishable, and this mortal body must put on immortality. (vv. 42–44, 51–53)

Regarding this imperishable body—one glorified and redeemed from all that inhibited it before—Paul says, "For we know that the whole creation has been groaning together in the pains of childbirth until now. And not only the creation, but we ourselves, who have the firstfruits of the Spirit, *groan inwardly* as we wait eagerly for adoption as sons, *the redemption of our bodies*" (Rom. 8:22–23).

There is far more we could say about the resurrection of the dead beyond these two points of our souls immediately being with Christ upon death and then eventually our souls being reunited with our glorified bodies in a literal bodily resurrection, but this gives us some starting handrails in affirming the variegated points the biblical data bring up about the resurrection of both the just and the unjust.

The Doctrine of Glorification

Glorification is the final crescendo in the grand symphony of salvation. If *justification* is our verdict of righteousness and *sanctification* is our transformation, then *glorification* completes the process by bringing us into the presence of God. Jason Alligood has defined the doctrine well, saying, "Glorification is the final stage of the Triune God's overarching work of salvation in believers in which he fully conforms them to the image of the glorified human nature of the Son and by which they will be totally free from sin and its effects."[3]

The doctrine of glorification is where we see the already and not yet of the Christian life come together in the glorious *now*. The already–not yet dichotomy may be new language for you, and it is worth taking a moment to discuss, since glorification is where the two meet. The way that God has designed Christian salvation is that there are riches of this great salvation we have *already* experienced. For example, if we have trusted in Christ by faith, we are *already* justified. Because of the merits our high priest imputed to us, God has *already* declared that we have satisfied every condition of the law, and there is nothing left for us to earn—we are *already* clean and pure. However, while we are *already* justified from our sin, we are *not yet* totally free from it. Our sin—while no longer putting us in a wrong relationship with God or inciting his wrath toward us—still plagues our day-to-day lives. It is still something we must mortify and put to death as we journey on this lifelong process of "[putting] off the old self" and "[putting] on the new self" (Eph. 4:22–24).

This is but one example where we see the already–not yet reality of the Christian life at play. We are *already* free from sin but *not yet* totally free from sin. We are *already* made holy but *not yet* living in perfect holiness. We are *already* redeemed but *not yet* living in complete redemption. We are *already* saved but *not yet* realizing the consummation of that salvation. There is much in God's economy of redemption that is this way—through the work of the Triune God, we have *already* tasted and seen so much grace, yet there is much glory and grace we have *not yet* come to fully obtain or realize. This

3. Jason B. Alligood, *Raised in Splendor: The Hope of Glorification for a Secular Age* (B&H, 2025), 12.

does not mean there is a chance it will not come to pass, as his promises are sure.

While glorification is a future promise for us today, it is as sure as past promises. This is why Paul can refer to glorification in the past tense: "Those whom he justified he also *glorified*" (Rom. 8:30). In God's sovereign economy, future grace is as trustworthy as past grace. However, there is still much in the *not yet* category we are awaiting in our pilgrimage. As a sample, consider the following chart.

The *Already* of the Christian Life	The *Not Yet* of Eschatology
We are already **saved** (Eph. 2:8).	We are not yet **fully saved** (Rom. 13:11; 1 Pet. 1:5).
We are already **justified** (Rom. 5:1).	We are not yet **finally vindicated** (Rom. 2:6–10).
We are already **adopted as God's children** (Gal. 4:5–6).	We have not yet received the **redemption of our bodies** that belongs to adoption (Rom. 8:23).
We already possess **eternal life** (John 5:24; 1 John 5:13).	We have not yet **fully experienced** eternal life in the age to come (Mark 10:30).
We are already **seated with Christ** in the heavenly places (Eph. 2:6).	We have not yet **been glorified and do not reign with him** (Rom. 8:17; 2 Tim. 2:12).
We already have the **Holy Spirit as our guarantee** (Eph. 1:13–14).	We have not yet realized our **full inheritance** from the Spirit (Col. 3:24; 1 Pet. 1:4).
We already have **victory over sin** (Rom. 6:6–7).	We have not yet conquered **sin's presence** (Rom. 7:21–25; Gal. 5:17).
We are already a **new creation** (2 Cor. 5:17).	We have not yet seen **creation's full renewal** (Rom. 8:19–20).
We are already citizens in the **kingdom of God** (Col. 1:13).	We have not yet received or seen the **kingdom in its fullness** (Matt. 6:10; Rev. 11:15).
We have already **seen God's glory in Christ** (John 14:9; 2 Cor. 4:6).	We have not yet enjoyed the **beatific vision** (1 Cor. 13:12; 1 John 3:2).
We are already **raised with Christ spiritually** (Eph. 2:5–6).	We have not yet been **physically and bodily resurrected** (1 Cor. 15:52).

To be glorified is not merely to be rescued from pain, though that will be a glorious aspect of it. Rather, to be glorified is to be the recipient of what God says in Ecclesiastes: "He has made everything beautiful in its time" (3:11). Glorification is the reversal of every fracture caused by the fall. It is not merely a return to the garden of Eden; it is even better than Eden. In glory, the Christian will be finally and fully conformed to the image of Christ. No sin, no sorrow, no shadow of shame can cling to the glorified Christian. No guilt has claim over them, no sadness will have air to breathe. The wounds of life will not simply be erased—they will be transfigured into markers of divine mercy.

In glory, our pain will turn to joy.
In glory, our sorrow will turn to singing.
In glory, our guilt will turn to freedom.
In glory, our waiting will turn to wonder.
In glory, our abuse will turn to victory.
In glory, our shame will turn to honor.
In glory, our death will lead to the fullness of life.

Glorification is where Eden's exiles gain a new permanent citizenship in the new heavens and new earth, and it is where those citizens get the thing their souls have been most longing for throughout their pilgrimage: God himself.

The Beatific Vision

Our desire—the deepest longing of our hearts, for God himself—will be finally and fully satisfied in the beatific vision. At a basic level, the beatific vision is the vision we will enjoy in heaven as we behold God's glory in the face of Christ in such a way that we cannot even dream of in this life. This vision of God's glory will lead to *beatitude*—or a supreme and preeminent gladness, joy, and blessedness—for all our eternal days. It is the vision that makes glad the soul and provides the realization that David was not kidding when he stated that "in your presence there is fullness of joy" (Ps. 16:11). Sam Parkison has served readers well with his definition of the beatific vision:

> The beatific vision is the telos of humanity: the vision of God the saints will enjoy in the eschaton. . . . The object of our contemplation by faith now (i.e., God in Christ) will be the object of this beatific vision forever—him whom we delight to behold by faith now we will continually delight to behold in glorified vision hereafter. . . . This vision is the full satiation of every creaturely desire and the absolute telos of the image-bearer. Every happiness that has partial fulfillment here will be realized in full in this vision, since this vision is the destination to which all natural desires lead.[4]

The doctrine of the beatific vision has had an interesting curve in church history. For centuries, the doctrine enjoyed a pride of place in the church's theological imagination; the beatific vision would have been among the first things to come to mind. This is why, to continue quoting Parkison, he can write, "What makes Heaven, Heaven? Christianity's resounding answer to that question throughout the centuries has been the beatific vision."[5] However, in more recent decades, the doctrine seems to have faded from prominence as the church considers what life across the Jordan will look like, to the degree that Michael Allen can write, "The doctrine of the beatific vision has dropped into oblivion."[6]

4. Samuel G. Parkison, *To Gaze Upon God: The Beatific Vision in Doctrine, Tradition, and Practice* (IVP Academic, 2024), 176.

5. Parkison, *Gaze Upon God*, 1.

6. Michael Allen, *Grounded in Heaven: Recentering the Christian Hope and Life on God* (Eerdmans, 2018), 59.

The hope of this eternal vision is consistent throughout the Scriptures, both Old and New Testament alike. Moses longs to see God's glory, the psalmist thirsts for the face of the Lord, John tells us the glory of the age to come is that "we shall see him as he is" (1 John 3:2). While it would be worthwhile to canvas all of Scripture with the aim to demonstrate the hope of God's people to be with and see their God, we will have to allow just a few references to suffice as testimony to this great doctrine. What follows are simply four passages showing this doctrine, to which I will add emphasis to illuminate it.

> One thing have I asked of the LORD,
>   that will I seek after:
> that I may dwell in the house of the LORD
>   all the days of my life,
> *to gaze upon the beauty of the* LORD
>   and to inquire in his temple. (Ps. 27:4)

> Love never ends. As for prophecies, they will pass away; as for tongues, they will cease; as for knowledge, it will pass away. For we know in part and we prophesy in part, but when the perfect comes, the *partial will pass away*. When I was a child, I spoke like a child, I thought like a child, I reasoned like a child. When I became a man, I gave up childish ways. *For now we see in a mirror dimly, but then face to face. Now I know in part; then I shall know fully*, even as I have been fully known. (1 Cor. 13:8–12)

> See what kind of love the Father has given to us, that we should be called children of God; and so we are. The reason why the world does not know us is that it did not know him. Beloved, we are God's children now, and what we will be has not yet appeared; but we know that when he appears we shall be like him, *because we shall see him as he is*. (1 John 3:1–2)

> Then the angel showed me the river of the water of life, bright as crystal, flowing from the throne of God and of the Lamb through the middle of the street of the city; also, on either side of the river, the tree of life with its twelve kinds of fruit, yielding its fruit each month. The leaves of the tree were for the healing of the nations. No longer will there by anything accursed, but the throne of God and of the Lamb will be in it, and his servants will worship him. *They will see his face*, and his name will be on their foreheads. And night will be no more. They will need no light of lamp or sun, for the Lord God will be their light, and they will reign forever and ever. (Rev. 22:1–5)

Among the most important emphases within the doctrine of the beatific vision is that it is God for whom our souls long. There are many things we ought to look forward to in heaven: the death of death, having every tear wiped from our eyes, the undoing of all injustice, the end of pain and suffering, the eradication of guilt, entering the fullness of rest, and more than our deepest dreams could fathom. However, as good as all these blessings are, what we want more than all of them is God himself. *He is our reward*. He is the One we are after in this pilgrimage of life. The beatific vision helps us not make a false dichotomy between the gifts of heaven and the giver of the gifts, for we get the fullness of heaven's gifts in the presence and vision of God himself. As Augustine writes, "God Himself, who is the author of virtue, shall there be its reward; for, as there is nothing greater or better, He has promised Himself."[7]

Every earthly beauty is but a shadow cast by the real beauty; every truth is grounded in the One who is truth; everything good on earth is but a participation in the real grounding of the One who is good. In this life our souls long for the true, the good, and the beautiful; in the next life our souls *get* the

7. Augustine, "The City of God," in *Nicene and Post-Nicene Fathers Second Series*, vol. 2, ed. Philip Schaff and Henry Wace (Hendrickson, 2007), 510.

One who is truth, goodness, and beauty as we behold him for all eternity.

Delighting in the Doctrine of Eschatology

The doctrine of eschatology answers one of the most persistent questions of the human heart: *Where is all of this going?* Scripture insists that the story of the world—and the story of our lives within it—is neither circular or unfinished but moving toward a promised end. Christian hope is rooted not in vague optimism or sentimental longing but in the sure faithfulness of God to complete what he has begun. When rightly understood, eschatology does not diminish the present life but dignifies it. It teaches us to live now in light of what will one day be fully revealed. To delight in eschatology, then, is to discover that the end gives shape, weight, and beauty to everything that comes before it. It is to that beauty that we turn as we seek to delight in the doctrine of eschatology.

Living with the End in Mind

I have a deep love for literature. In fact, had I not pursued theology as a vocation, I would have chosen something in the field of English or poetry. My love for fiction is rivaled only by my love for coffee. There are precious few hours of my life when there is neither a novel nor a cup of coffee within arm's reach. One morning, I was sitting in a coffee shop, finishing up a novel for my long-standing fiction book club. As I neared the end of the novel, the novelist—the great Marilynne Robinson—had a line that I was not prepared for. Robinson was writing about fractures that exist in families and the deep wounds they can cause, something I know from personal experience. In that scene, with the twists and turns of family hurt behind her, the main character asks a penetrating question that is the hope not just for fractured families but for all fractured souls: "What are all these fragments for if not to be knitted up in the end finally?"[8]

This question hit me not only for its literary beauty but also because this is what it looks like to live with the end in mind. We know, as Christians, that God will be faithful to take the many fragments of our lives and knit them into something glorious in the end. This is not mere wishful thinking but the Christian's hope.

To live with the end in mind is to know that God is up to something and that this whole thing is going somewhere. Living with the eschaton in view charges every dull moment of our day-to-day with meaning. It is to know that there are no ordinary people; rather, all people who have ever lived are made in the image of God. We are all on our way to an end in which we will stand before him either as our delight or as our destruction. Living with the end in mind is to know likewise that there are no ordinary moments but that, with each successive passing moment, we are one breath closer to seeing God and being in the fullness of joy forevermore. Rather than causing an escapist mentality in which we simply live for the next life, living with the end in mind causes the meaning of this life to erupt in truth, goodness, and beauty.

We may hear it said from well-meaning Christians, from time to time, that "we should not be so heavenly minded that we are no earthly good." It is well documented elsewhere, but I will join the chorus of voices here to say that this piece of advice, as well-meaning as it is, seems misinformed. In fact, I find that C. S. Lewis is correct when he says instead, "If you read history, you will find that the Christians who did most for the present world were just those who thought most of the next."[9]

8. Marilynne Robinson, *Housekeeping* (Picador, 2020), 92.
9. C. S. Lewis, *Mere Christianity* (HarperCollins, 1980), 134.

One passage of Scripture strikes me as particularly beautiful as relates to living our day-to-day lives with the end in mind. First Peter is a book for suffering. The recipients of Peter's letter are exiles who have likely lost much and suffered even more. Much of what Peter writes is aimed at producing steadfastness during suffering. This is why he writes, "In this you rejoice, though now for a little while, if necessary, you have been grieved by various trials, so that the tested genuineness of your faith—more precious than gold that perishes though it is tested by fire—may be found to result in praise and glory and honor at the revelation of Jesus Christ" (1 Pet. 1:6–7). Notice that Peter puts the current suffering of the exiled Christians in light of the coming of Jesus Christ, which gives them their proper perspective. Peter writes as one with the end in mind for those he wants to live with the end in mind.

Perhaps we see this best in Peter's writings when he tells his readers, "The end of all things is at hand" (4:7) and then instructs them how to live. You may expect what follows that kind of setup to be dramatic, right? If we were to finish that sentence, we may say things like, "The end of all things is at hand . . . so live to the fullest, check off items on that bucket list, do the thing you have been dreaming of doing," and so on. However, Peter's advice for those who are living in the end is *remarkably normal*.

> The end of all things is at hand; therefore be self-controlled and sober-minded for the sake of your prayers. Above all, keep loving one another earnestly, since love covers a multitude of sins. Show hospitality to one another without grumbling. As each has received a gift, use it to serve one another, as good stewards of God's varied grace. (vv. 7–10)

Are you serious? The end of the world is coming . . . so *be sober-minded*? *Be hospitable*? *Love one another*? *Be prayerful*?

These things seem remarkably normal for a passage that begins by invoking the end of all things! But this is what living with the end in mind will do for us. If we live with eschatology in mind and remind our souls that one day all of the not yet will smash into the already, it will cause even ordinary and regular moments and movements to have more meaning than we could imagine. If we live with that feeling in the back of our minds, that *there has got to be more than this*, we are probably right, but what likely needs to change is not all our circumstances but living our regular rhythms in light of the end.

Cultivated Souls and Our Life Across the Jordan

Few things bring more wonder and simultaneously more frustration than Solomon's words that God has "put eternity into man's heart" (Eccles. 3:11). Even the sentiment in the above paragraph—*there has got to be more than this*—is the realization that our hearts contain what this life will never encompass. We will always feel a touch like exiles here in this earthly life because we simply are not yet home. God put eternity in our hearts, and it provides a consistent reminder that we are made for life eternal with him.

As we have discussed in this chapter, we will spend that next life getting to realize David's greatest desire—"One thing have I asked of the Lord, that will I seek after: That I may dwell in the house of the Lord all the days of my life, to gaze upon the beauty of the Lord and to inquire in his temple" (Ps. 27:4). David's deepest desire is our future. We will gaze upon the beauty of the Lord all our days.

With this in mind, if we are going to spend the life hereafter gazing at the beauty of the Lord and ever pressing further into truth, goodness, and beauty, then surely we should begin *now* by cultivating souls that can actually give sustained attention to that which is good, true, and beautiful in this life. We can each participate in our everlasting vocation of gazing at the beauty of the Lord in the hereafter by seeking to turn our mind's eye to the Lord's beauty *now*. With whatever days he gives us and at whatever starting point we currently reside, we can pick up the great task of seeing beauty. Moreover, in a world of fractured attention spans, with a million competing voices vying for our affection, and in an age when shallowness is gravity, may we do the hard work of cultivating our souls toward Christlikeness so we can have sustained attention on who God is and what he is doing in the world. This is just one more way in which our day-to-day life today can be impacted by the world to come. To be sure, this point may not be as significant as the other two in this delight section, but it is one that resonates with both me and my students semester after semester.

Further Up, Further In

I want to end by bringing together two doctrines, one we considered at the beginning of this work and one we considered here at the end: divine incomprehensibility and the beatific vision.

These two doctrines come together to form an important question in the field of eschatology—namely, does the vision we enjoy in heaven, the beatific vision, mean that we will get to comprehend God in heaven? Will we know God in an exhaustive way in eternal life, since we will see him in a way we cannot fathom right now? I wish I could answer this question with a yes. Part of me wishes I could tell you that in the afterlife, we will know all there is to know about God, and that will be the joy of heaven. However, I am convinced the answer is a resounding no. No, the beatific vision does not mean that we will comprehend God. This is profoundly good news—in fact, this is such profoundly good news that any other way of ending this chapter on eschatology or ending this book in general would fall short by comparison.

The reason God is incomprehensible to us is not due to God being merely bigger than us in some way such that with enough time we could comprehend him. God is incomprehensible due to the Creator-creature distinction we discussed earlier. He is the One who spoke all things into being; we are those who were spoken into being. He is the One who is unchanging, who has life in himself. He is the plenitude of life who has always existed. We are finite, constantly changing, remarkably needy, and here for but a moment. God is not merely bigger than us by degree but altogether different from us in kind—he is the Creator; we are the creature. This is significant because that distinction will not be undone in heaven. We will be glorified creatures, yes, but we will nevertheless still be creatures.

There is an eternity of beauty in this reality. I have written elsewhere on this exact reality:

> The fate that awaits those united to the Son is a sight through the Son in which the redeemed will get to ever apprehend the beauty of God's essence without comprehension or exhaustion. While it may seem counterintuitive, not arriving at a state of comprehension—even while partaking in the beatific vision—is the good news of the eschaton. For it means that those perfections which we adore most about God will never run out of material even with everlasting growth in apprehension.[10]

10. Ronni Kurtz, *Light Unapproachable: Divine Incomprehensibility and the Task of Theology* (IVP Academic, 2024), 134. Samuel Parkison makes a near identical point:

> All creaturely existence is a gift, *including* creaturely limitations. In that blessed vision, our comprehension and vision and delight, which are all *finite*, will be perpetually maximized. And as our capacity for comprehension and vision expands, so will our delight. In other words, the very limitations we are tempted to bemoan create the possibility of never ending delight, where each level of enjoyment is topped by the next—forever. This upward spiral into deeper beatific communion with the Trinity will never be exhausted—because we are finite, and the object of our delight is infinite, our blessedness will increase forever. "In your presence there is

Do not miss the beauty here: On that great day when we are ushered into the presence of the Lord and finally get to enjoy the church's great hope—the sight and presence of God—you and I will see him in a way we could never even begin to understand in this life. And yet, even with the sight of the beatific vision, we will *never* exhaust the glories of God. Moreover, we will have not only the beatific vision but also an eternity to explore him—and *still* we will not exhaust his excellencies. This is the death of any idea that heaven may be boring. The glory of God in the face of Jesus Christ will ever beckon us further into inexhaustible beauty.

This understanding should ignite our souls in delight. It is in this idea of ever apprehending the beauty of the Lord without ever exhausting the beauty of the Lord that we really see the truth of one of C. S. Lewis's most profound lines: "Further up and further in." This is the victorious cry of the characters of Narnia as, in the final book of the series, the members of Aslan's army finally get to enter the true and better Narnia. As they enter the Narnian equivalent of the afterlife, they feel themselves filled with a deep desire to run—to move further up and further in to the true country their hearts have so long desired. Reepicheep cries out, "Welcome, in the Lion's name. Come further up and further in." Mr. Tumnus calls, "The further up and the further in you go, the bigger everything gets. The inside is larger than the outside."[11] Emeth, and Jewel, and Farsight, and the Unicorn all beseech one another—*further up and further in.*

The power of Lewis's line stems from the fact that he is writing about something he has no jurisdiction over. Lewis, like you and me, could not imagine the wonders of heaven, which is why "further up and further in" is a perfect way to express

fullness of joy; at your right hand are pleasures forevermore" (Ps. 16:11). (Parkison, *Gaze Upon God*, 20)

11. C. S. Lewis, *The Last Battle* (HarperCollins, 1984), 202–8.

it. We are not sure what exactly will be there at the end of all things, but we know *who* will be there—God himself. If it is he whom our souls are pilgriming toward, then when we finally arrive on that great shore, I am confident the cry of our hearts will indeed be *further up and further in*.

Acknowledgments

A refrain I find myself often repeating to my students is that theology is never meant to be done alone. By God's kindness, that is true of this book, as there is an embarrassment of riches in my life—from colleagues, administrators, friends, and family who deserve much thanks for this book.

First, I'd like to thank my editors at Baker Books, especially Eddie LaRow and Lindsey Spoolstra. Eddie has been a friend for years, and I am thankful he took the risk on me not just as a friend but now as an author. Editors sometimes push for a conciseness that can bring beauty to the altar of sacrifice; Eddie pushed me as an author to try to capture not only the true but also the beautiful. (And, fine, conciseness as well.) It was a joy to work with him. Lindsey Spoolstra is a gifted editor, and I am thankful for her fingerprints throughout this book. I have no doubt the book you hold is better for her having spent time with it. Thanks also to Brian Vos for his many encouragements in the process and for entrusting me to pursue a book geared between the academy and the local church—I am increasingly thankful for publishers like him willing to step into that space.

This book crossed the finish line during my first semester back at Midwestern Baptist Theological Seminary. While there are many wonderful people at Midwestern worthy of thanks, I particularly want to thank our president, Jason K. Allen, and our provost, Jason G. Duesing. Serving students through theology is a dream job, and there is no chance I would have obtained this vocation I love so much without the many years of help from these two. Thanks as well to the friends and colleagues who had to hear too much about this book over the years I was writing it, including Patrick Schreiner, Thomas Kidd, Peter Gurry, John Meade, Andrew King, Don Whitney, Jared Bumpers, and Samuel Parkison.

It should be no surprise to anyone who reads chapter 9 that I have a high view of the local church. During the writing of this manuscript, I transitioned membership from Trinity Church in Dayton, Ohio, to Emmaus Church in Kansas City, Missouri, as I became a professor at Midwestern Seminary. Therefore, I'd like to thank my elders, both at Trinity and at Emmaus, for watching over my soul as I wrote these words: Chris Bernstein, Glen Higgins, and Ed VanderBush at Trinity, and Tyler Greene, Patrick Schreiner, Sean Stone, and Kirk Metzger at Emmaus. Thanks for shepherding my family and for making sure our theology is always a theology for life.

Finally, I want to thank my family. My dad, Ron Kurtz Sr., read every word of this manuscript as he has with every book I have written to date. His presence in my corner means more than I could say in a single acknowledgments section. I love you, Dad. As always, next to me for hours while writing this manuscript was my best friend and family member, Josh Brown. He and his wife, Meagan Brown, are among the greatest gifts to my wife and me this side of heaven. Finally, my wife and our two children deserve the most thanks. My wife Kristen is more supportive of my writing life than I deserve. Often, chapters, pages, and even sentences come only because of her sacrifices.

She gives deep meaning to our ordinary rhythms, and it is often the beauty she has cultivated in our lives from which I write. My two children, Finley and Cohen, have been exactly what I needed while writing this book: themselves. Often, wrestling with them or chasing them around the house was the exact thing I needed to keep going.

This book is dedicated to my son, Cohen Haddon Kurtz. I wrote most of this manuscript during the first few years of his life. He is a joy to me, and it is the privilege of a lifetime to be his dad. I pray he will find in Jesus the greatest love of his life and the greatest adventure of his days. May you have a theological imagination that takes you ever into the true, the good, and the beautiful. I love you, son.

Ronni Kurtz
Kansas City, Missouri

Ronni Kurtz (PhD, Midwestern Baptist Theological Seminary) is an assistant professor of systematic theology at Midwestern Baptist Theological Seminary and Spurgeon College. He is the author or coauthor of a number of books, including *Light Unapproachable*, *Proclaiming the Triune God*, *Fruitful Theology*, and *No Shadow of Turning*. Previously he taught theology at Cedarville University and also planted and pastored a church for eight years. He lives in Kansas City, Missouri, with his wife and two children.

Connect with Ronni:

@ronnikurtz

@RonniKurtz